York Notes Rapid Revision

Power and Conflict Poetry Anthology

AQA GCSE English Literature

Written by David Grant

Pearson

YORK PRESS

YORK PRESS
322 Old Brompton Road, London SW5 9JH

PEARSON EDUCATION LIMITED
80 Strand, London, WC2R 0RL

© Librairie du Liban *Publishers* 2019

10 9 8 7 6 5 4 3 2 1
ISBN 978–1–2922–7092–0

Phototypeset by Ken Vail Graphic Design
Printed in Slovakia

Text credits:
'Storm on the Island' from *Poems 1965-1975* by Seamus Heaney. Copyright © 1980 Seamus Heaney. Reprinted by permission of Farrar, Straus and Giroux and Faber and Faber Ltd. 'Bayonet Charge' from *Collected Poems* by Ted Hughes. Copyright © 2003 by The Estate of Ted Hughes. Reprinted by permission of Farrar, Straus and Giroux and Faber and Faber Ltd. 'Remains' by Simon Armitage from *The Not Dead*, 2008, published by Pomona, reproduced by kind permission of Pomona. 'Poppies' by Jane Weir, copyright © Templar Poetry from *The Way I Dressed During the Revolution* (Templar Poetry, 2010). 'War Photographer' from *Standing Female Nude* by Carol Ann Duffy. Published by Anvil Press Poetry, 1985. Copyright © Carol Ann Duffy. Reproduced by permission of the author c/o Rogers, Coleridge & White Ltd., 20 Powis Mews, London W11 1JN. 'Tissue' by Imtiaz Dharker from *The Terrorist at My Table* (Bloodaxe Books, 2006), reprinted with permission of Bloodaxe Books on behalf of the author, www.bloodaxebooks.com. 'The Emigrée' by Carol Rumens, reproduced by permission of the author. 'Checking Out Me History' copyright © John Agard 1996, reproduced by kind permission of John Agard c/o Caroline Sheldon Literary Agency Ltd. 'Kamikaze' by Beatrice Garland, copyright © Templar Poetry, from *The Invention of Fireworks* (Templar Poetry, 2013)

Photo credits:
Bill McKelvie/Shutterstock for page 5 middle / Everett-Art/Shutterstock for page 9 middle / Cortyn/Shutterstock for page 14 middle / Granger Historical Picture Archive/Alamy for page 18 middle and page 66 middle / Lebrecht Music & Arts/Alamy for page 22 middle / Jan Jacob Trip/Shutterstock for page 26 middle / Lemonakis Antonis/Shutterstock for page 29 middle and page 74 middle / igs942/© iStock for page 33 middle and page 70 bottom / Getmilitaryphotos/Shutterstock for page 37 bottom / Africa Studio/Shutterstock for page 38 middle / Rene Baars/Shutterstock for page 41 bottom / Paul Doyle/Alamy for page 42 middle / andipantz/© iStock for page 45 middle / Attitude/© iStock for page 49 bottom / FangXiaNuo/© iStock for page 50 middle / Shanina/© iStock for page 53 middle / Everett Historical/Shutterstock for page 58 middle / Keith Tarrier/Shutterstock for page 61 bottom / buritora/Shutterstock for page 62 middle / Ed Samuel/Shutterstock for page 68 bottom

CONTENTS

OZYMANDIAS by Percy Bysshe Shelley

This poem was first published in 1819. It describes the ruins of a vast statue that a traveller has seen in the desert. In the **Romantic period**, it was very fashionable to travel to Egypt to explore the buildings and artefacts of its ancient civilisation.

Language choices from **semantic field** of deterioration and decay used throughout the poem (see also ll. 12–13)

Imperfect rhyme supports **themes** of decay and corruption

Harsh-sounding **alliteration** foregrounds Pharaoh's cruelty

Transience of political regimes: Ozymandias's passions – his arrogance – survive in the ruined statue but his 'works' do not

Irony through **juxtaposition** of 'passions' and 'lifeless things' – highlighting decay and the passing of time

1 I met a traveller from an antique land
   Who said: Two vast and trunkless legs of stone
   Stand in the desert. Near them on the sand,
   Half sunk, a shatter'd visage lies, whose frown
5 And wrinkled lip and sneer of cold command
   Tell that its sculptor well those passions read
   Which yet survive, stamp'd on these lifeless things,
   The hand that mock'd them and the heart that fed;
   And on the pedestal these words appear:
10 'My name is Ozymandias, king of kings:
   Look on my works, ye Mighty, and despair!'
   Nothing beside remains. Round the decay
   Of that colossal wreck, boundless and bare,
   The lone and level sands stretch far away.

Ambiguity – suggests Ozymandias's hand mocked his people, and his heart fed on their suffering? Or suggests the sculptor's hand mocked Ozymandias's face?

Irony through structure – placing this immediately after grandiose claim shows its emptiness

Turning point mid line disrupts **sonnet** form and echoes subject matter: the decay of the statue and the breakdown of Ozymandias's power

Alliteration highlights image of vast, unforgiving desert in which the fallen statue lies shattered and forgotten

Power of nature: the desert endures; Ozymandias's power does not

Imperative verb suggests his power and arrogance

End-stopped lines, in contrast to frequent **enjambment** in rest of poem, add emphasis to this grandiose claim

4

What is the poem's setting?

- The poem describes what remains of a **huge statue**, probably of **Ramses II**, in the middle of **a vast desert**.
- Shelley highlights the **emptiness** of the desert's **'lone and level sands'**. He contrasts it with Ozymandias's **proud boast** of **'works'** that are intended to make his enemies **'despair'**, but which have long since **decayed** and disappeared.

What is the poem about?

- Shelley describes the fallen, decayed statue of **an arrogant king** which is all that remains of him.
- The description of the statue is given in **reported speech**: an account given by **'a traveller from an antique land'**.

- The description of the statue's face suggests a callous, **ruthless** leader.
- The **theme of power** is highlighted in the arrogance of the inscription on the statue. The **temporary nature of power** and achievement are highlighted in the statue's **decay**.
- Shelley disrupts the traditional sonnet form, perhaps implying **disrespect** for those in power who make the rules.

Five Key things about the language

1. Shelley's language choices throughout the poem highlight the statue's disintegration.
2. Shelley creates a formal and dramatic **tone** suggesting Ozymandias's grandeur and the imposing sight of the fallen statue in the barren desert.
3. Shelley uses irony to contrast the statue's arrogant inscription with what remains of Ozymandias's power and his **'works'**.
4. The use of imperative verbs in the statue's inscription highlights Ozymandias's arrogance and vanity.
5. Shelley uses alliteration and enjambment in the final lines to highlight the vast emptiness of the desert where Ozymandias's **'works'** once stood.

Five key quotations

1. Fallen statue: **'a shatter'd visage'** (l. 4). Time has destroyed the face.

2. Ozymandias's face: **'frown/And wrinkled lip and sneer of cold command'** ll. 4–5). The words **'sneer'** and **'cold'** suggest a ruthless and unemotional ruler.

3. Arrogant inscription: **'Look on my works, ye Mighty, and despair!'** (l. 11). Ozymandias seems to be taunting other kings, arrogantly boasting of his superiority.

4. Human power is temporary: **'Nothing beside remains.'** (l. 12). A short sentence emphasises that Ozymandias's power and achievements have crumbled and disappeared.

5. Power of nature: **'The lone and level sands stretch far away.'** (l. 14). The timelessness and power of nature contrast with the temporary power of kings.

Note it!

Compare Shelley's depiction of Ozymandias with Browning's presentation of the Duke in 'My Last Duchess'. What does each poet suggest about the nature of power?

Exam focus

How can I write about the theme of power?

You can analyse Shelley's depiction of Ozymandias to explore his presentation of power.

> Shelley describes the face of Ozymandias to imply the kind of ruler he was. For example, words such as 'sneer', 'frown' and 'cold' clearly suggest his disrespectful and ruthless attitude. However, before this, Shelley highlights that the statue's face is now 'shatter'd' and 'Half sunk' in the desert sand, suggesting how meaningless his arrogance and power are now, centuries later.

Topic sentence makes clear point

Carefully chosen words support the point

Signals a contrasting idea

Comments on the cumulative effect

Now you try!

Finish this paragraph about another **theme**. Use one of the quotations from the list.

The poet suggests that the power of nature is greater than any human power. This is shown in ....

My progress　Needs more work ☐　Getting there ☐　Sorted! ☐

SPECIAL FOCUS 1: Sound and rhythm

What are sound and rhythm?

- Poets often choose **specific words** because of the effect of **particular letter sounds**, e.g. words beginning with **plosive** 'p's or 'b's can sound harsh and aggressive.
- The **rhythm** of a poem is created by the **positioning of words** to create **stresses or beats**.

How do I identify these in a poem like 'Ozymandias'?

- Read the poem **aloud**, looking for words which are given **emphasis** by the poem's rhythm, e.g. **'vast'** in l. 2, **'lip'**, **'sneer'** and **'cold'** in l. 5.
- Think about how the poet **disrupts the rhythm** of the poem, e.g. to draw attention, and give emphasis, to the arrogant inscription on the statue in ll. 10 and 11.
- Look at the poet's use of **punctuation**, e.g. how the final sentence slows the rhythm as the empty desert sands stretch into the distance.
- Think about ways in which the **sound** of words adds to their impact, e.g. the harsh **alliteration** of 'cold command'.

Exam focus

How can I write about sound and rhythm? AO2

You could use **verbs** and **adjectives** related to sound and rhythm:
e.g. *regular, irregular, constant, disrupt, harsh, soft, rapid, slow, emphatic, dramatic.*

In the second part of the poem, Shelley disrupts its regular rhythm with the short sentence 'Nothing beside remains.', creating an emphatic contrast to the arrogant inscription on the statue. Then, by spreading the final long sentence over three lines, he slows the poem's rhythm to suggest the endless emptiness where Ozymandias's kingdom once stood.

Evidence from the poem

Rhythm words

How rhythm changes

Now you try!

Think about the other poems in the cluster. Do any of them use sound or rhythm to add emphasis to their ideas?

LONDON by William Blake

This poem is taken from William Blake's *Songs of Experience* published in 1794, shortly after the French Revolution. It describes the rapidly growing city as a place blighted by the impact of the Industrial Revolution: a city of inequality and oppression.

Iambic tetrameter (broken at ll. 4, 9–12, and 14–15) creates a heavy **rhythm**

Power structures: every aspect of the city is owned by people in power, even its streets and river

Oppression: everyone in the city is affected with 'marks' of misery

Repetition of 'marks' emphasises people's suffering

Repetition of 'every' highlights universal effects of oppression

Metaphor conveys entrapment in psychological chains

Definite article suggests the soldier and chimney sweep represent sections of society

Regular **rhyme** scheme could suggest drudgery of everyday life

1 I wander through each chartered street,
   Near where the chartered Thames does flow,
   And mark in every face I meet
   Marks of weakness, marks of woe.

5 In every cry of every man,
   In every infant's cry of fear,
   In every voice, in every ban,
   The mind-forged manacles I hear:

   How the chimney-sweeper's cry
10 Every black'ning church appalls,
   And the hapless soldier's sigh
   Runs in blood down palace walls.

   But most through midnight streets I hear
   How the youthful harlot's curse
15 Blasts the new-born infant's tear,
   And blights with plagues the marriage hearse.

Plosive alliterated verbs imply violence

Juxtaposition of 'harlot' and 'infant' suggests the corruption of innocence

Oxymoron suggests a link between marriage and death

Emotive vocabulary creates a dramatic, critical **tone**

What is the poem's setting?

- The poem presents a **negative view** of the city of **London** and **its people**.
- Much of the city is **'chartered'** meaning it is **owned** by the **wealthy and powerful**, while the poor live a life of **misery and oppression**.

What is the poem about?

- The speaker describes a **journey** through the streets of London. The poem's largely regular rhyme scheme and heavy rhythm suggest a slow walk and reflect the depressing sights he encounters.
- He notes the **suffering** of the city's people.
- He suggests that the **Church** is unsympathetic to this suffering and that **revolution** is imminent, describing blood running down palace walls.
- The final image of **cursing prostitutes** and **crying babies** creates a powerful impression of degradation and corruption.
- The **theme** of **oppression** is highlighted throughout the poem, e.g. the speaker hears **'mind-forged manacles'** in every **'cry'** and **'voice'** of the city.

Five key things about the language

1. Blake uses repetition to highlight the universal suffering of the people of London.
2. He uses a range of vocabulary related to suffering and anguish, e.g. **'weakness'**, **'woe'**, **'cry'**, **'fear'**, **'sigh'**, **'tear'**.
3. Alliteration adds dramatic emphasis to Blake's choices of emotive vocabulary, e.g. **'mind-forged manacles'**, **'Blasts'**, **'blights'**.
4. Blake refers to those in power indirectly, e.g. the wealthy are implied in **'each chartered street'**; royalty in the **'palace'**; religion in the **'church'**. This focuses our attention on the people of London and their suffering.
5. His use of shocking **imagery**, with phrases such as **'youthful harlot'**, suggests a city of corruption and potential violence.

Five key quotations

1. **Power and wealth:** 'each chartered street ... the chartered Thames' (ll. 1–2). Even the city's streets and river are owned by the wealthy.
2. **Suffering:** 'Marks of weakness, marks of woe' (l. 4). **Repetition** emphasises the impact of suffering on the people of London.
3. **Children:** 'every infant's cry of fear' (l. 6). This is one of two **emotive** references to the suffering of innocent children.
4. **Oppression:** 'mind-forged manacles' (l. 8). The metaphor suggests oppressive chains created by and imprisoning people's minds.
5. **Conflict:** 'blood down palace walls' (l. 12). The image suggests possible revolution.

Note it!

Compare the depiction of suffering in 'London' with Owen's depiction of it in 'Exposure'. Are the vocabulary choices similar in any way?

Exam focus

How can I write about the theme of conflict? AO1 AO2

You can analyse Blake's use of imagery to explore the theme of conflict.

Blake creates shocking images of conflict in the poem. For example, he depicts 'blood' running down 'palace walls', suggesting a violent and bloody revolution. Furthermore, he hints at conflict in the lives of the people of London, juxtaposing a 'youthful harlot's curse' and a 'new-born infant's tear', implying that the innocence of children is soon corrupted. The impression these images create is of a city of conflict, suffering and degradation.

- Topic sentence makes clear point
- Carefully chosen evidence supports point
- Signals a developed analysis
- Sums up and refers back to theme

Now you try!

Finish this paragraph about another **theme**. Use one of the quotations from the list.

Throughout the poem, Blake highlights the suffering of the people. He describes .....

My progress Needs more work ☐ Getting there ☐ Sorted! ☐

SPECIAL FOCUS 2: Voice and viewpoint

What are voice and viewpoint?

- The **voice** in a poem is the **speaker** or **narrator**.
- The **viewpoint** is the **perspective** that the speaker offers on the theme.

How do I identify these in a poem like 'London'?

- Sometimes, a clear **narrative** voice is identified in a poem.
- In 'London', a **voice** is created using 'I', but we can't assume this is the poet's own voice. Even when we know the poem is autobiographical, or reflects the poet's own views, the poet has still created a **persona**.
- **Viewpoint** can be **complex** to identify, e.g. is Blake simply describing the people of London, is he criticising them, or does he blame their suffering on those in positions of power?
- Consider the **vocabulary** used, e.g. in 'London', Blake draws on the **semantic field** of pain and suffering to describe the people of the city, implying that he sympathises with them.
- Examine the **mood** and **tone**, e.g. the slow, heavy **rhythm** and vocabulary choices create a sombre mood, suggesting the speaker's distress at the scenes he sees and hears.

Exam focus

How can I write about voice and viewpoint? (AO2)

You could use **adjectives** or **adverbs** to identify viewpoint: *thoughtfully, enthusiastic, sympathetic, sombre, cautiously.*

Blake uses emotive vocabulary such as 'woe', 'fear', 'cry' and 'sigh' to describe the people of London, highlighting the misery of their lives and a viewpoint which is sympathetic to their suffering but critical of those in power who are responsible for it.

> Evidence from the language

> Impact of viewpoint on the reader

> Voice/viewpoint indicators

Now you try!

Think about the other poems in the cluster. Which are written in the first **person**? How does the poet suggest the speaker's voice and viewpoint?

Extract from THE PRELUDE by William Wordsworth

This is an extract from an extremely long autobiographical poem which Wordsworth began writing aged 28 and left unfinished at his death 52 years later. Many of the episodes in the poem describe journeys the poet undertakes and their impact upon him.

Personification of nature, at first presented as a benign female force

First **person** speaker for this autobiographical **narrative** poem

Blank verse and frequent **enjambment** throughout create a reflective, thoughtful **mood**

Word choice and position emphasise an impulsive decision

Foreshadows the power of the mountain, though the **tone** here is light

Adverb shows nature's effortless beauty

Nature's beauty is transient

The vastness of nature

Simile suggests apparently effortless movement

1   One summer evening (led by her) I found
    A little boat tied to a willow tree
    Within a rocky cove, its usual home.
    Straight I unloosed her chain, and stepping in
5   Pushed from the shore. It was an act of stealth
    And troubled pleasure, nor without the voice
    Of mountain-echoes did my boat move on;
    Leaving behind her still, on either side,
    Small circles glittering idly in the moon,
10 Until they melted all into one track
    Of sparkling light. But now, like one who rows,
    Proud of his skill, to reach a chosen point
    With an unswerving line, I fixed my view
    Upon the summit of a craggy ridge,
15 The horizon's utmost boundary; far above
    Was nothing but the stars and the grey sky.
    She was an elfin pinnace; lustily
    I dipped my oars into the silent lake,
    And, as I rose upon the stroke, my boat
20 Went heaving through the water like a swan;
    When, from behind that craggy steep till then

The power of the natural world

Nature, no longer female or benign, is presented as threatening

Repetition suggests and emphasises speaker's fear

Harsh consonant sounds and repetition suggest speaker's fear and helplessness

> The horizon's bound, a huge peak, black and huge,
> As if with voluntary power instinct,
> Upreared its head. I struck and struck again,
> 25 And growing still in stature the grim shape
> Towered up between me and the stars, and still,
> For so it seemed, with purpose of its own
> And measured motion like a living thing,
> Strode after me. With trembling oars I turned,
> 30 And through the silent water stole my way
> Back to the covert of the willow tree;
> There in her mooring-place I left my bark, –
> And through the meadows homeward went, in grave
> And serious mood; but after I had seen
> 35 That spectacle, for many days, my brain
> Worked with a dim and undetermined sense
> Of unknown modes of being; o'er my thoughts
> There hung a darkness, call it solitude
> Or blank desertion. No familiar shapes
> 40 Remained, no pleasant images of trees,
> Of sea or sky, no colours of green fields;
> But huge and mighty forms, that do not live
> Like living men, moved slowly through the mind
> By day, and were a trouble to my dreams.

Personification used again to create a sense of threat

Speaker returns to his starting point, though mood has changed dramatically

Adjectives create sense of fear and uncertainty

Semantic field of depression shows the effect on the speaker

Repetition of negative phrases suggests the experience is dominating the speaker's thoughts

Return to key word used earlier shows enduring power of fear

The imagination is powerful, but the power of nature can overwhelm the human imagination

13

Extract from THE PRELUDE by William Wordsworth

What is the poem's setting?

- The poem describes a **journey in a rowing boat** across a lake in the **Lake District**, surrounded by mountains.
- The poet focuses much of his **description of the setting** on the **night sky**, both above the boat and reflected in the water, creating a strong impression of **space** and **openness**.

What is the poem about?

- This **narrative** poem tells the story of the speaker **finding a boat and taking it**. He rows across the **lake** at **night**.
- At first the speaker admires his surroundings and is pleased with his **skill in rowing**.
- He is **surprised and disturbed** by the sudden, **threatening** appearance of a **'huge peak, black and huge'**.
- He **turns the boat** and **returns** it to the edge of the lake where he found it.
- The **theme** of **nature** is explored in the impact of the natural world upon the speaker. Though he admires nature's beauty, he is **overwhelmed** and **disturbed** by its power in the **'huge peak'** that becomes **'a trouble to my dreams'** for several days afterwards.

Five key things about the language

1. The peaceful night and beauty of nature are suggested in highly focused descriptive detail, e.g. **'Small circles glittering idly'**.
2. Wordsworth suggests an unsettled **mood** at the start of the poem, describing feelings of **'troubled pleasure'**, while **'the voice/Of mountain-echoes'** **foreshadow** the disturbing **personification** of nature that follows.
3. The mountain is personified as a threatening force.
4. Wordsworth uses **repetition** to emphasise the scale and power of the mountain.
5. He contrasts the beauty of nature with its power as **'huge and mighty forms'** overwhelm memories of **'pleasant images of trees'** and **'green fields'**.

Five key quotations

1. Beauty of nature: 'sparkling light' (l. 11). The **adjective** 'sparkling' suggests an almost magical beauty.
2. The mountain: 'a huge peak, black and huge' (l. 22). Repetition of the adjective 'huge' suggests the scale of the mountain, dominating the speaker's thoughts.
3. The power of nature: 'Strode after me' (l. 29). This personification presents nature as a threatening, dangerous force.
4. Beauty is forgotten: 'no pleasant images of trees,/ ... no colours of green fields' (ll. 40–1). Repeating 'no' stresses nature's power in destroying the speaker's memories of its beauty.
5. Disturbing nature: 'mighty forms, that do not live/Like living men, moved slowly through the mind' (ll. 42–3). The ominous image suggests the powerful impact the experience has had on the speaker.

Note it!

Compare Wordsworth's depiction of the natural world with its destructive power as shown in the conditions described in 'Exposure'. Do both poets show its impact in a similar way?

Exam focus

How can I write about the use of personification? AO2

You can write about how Wordsworth uses personification to explore nature's power.

> Wordsworth personifies the mountain to suggest the dramatic effect it has on him. For example, he describes how the mountain 'Upreared its head', and then 'Strode after me', presenting the mountain as a dangerous and threatening monster. This power is further shown as the sight of it makes him turn back and leave the 'sparkling' beauty of the lake.

Topic sentence makes clear point

Carefully chosen quotations

Signals a developed analysis

Links and contrasts two different aspects of the poem

Now you try!

Finish this paragraph about another theme. Use one of the quotations from the list.

The poet also suggests the lasting effect that this disturbing experience of nature had on him. At the end of the poem he ....

MY LAST DUCHESS by Robert Browning

This poem was written in the nineteenth century but is a **dramatic monologue** in the **voice** of the Duke of Ferrara who lived in the sixteenth century. It can be read as a criticism of the powerful and wealthy and their attitudes to status, women and marriage.

Rhyming couplets in **iambic pentameter** – though **enjambment** creates the **rhythm** of natural spoken language

Ferrara

1 That's my last Duchess painted on the wall,
Looking as if she were alive. I call
That piece a wonder, now: Frà Pandolf's hands
Worked busily a day, and there she stands.
5 Will't please you sit and look at her? I said
'Frà Pandolf' by design, for never read
Strangers like you that pictured countenance,
The depth and passion of its earnest glance,
But to myself they turned (since none puts by
10 The curtain I have drawn for you, but I)
And seemed as they would ask me, if they durst,
How such a glance came there; so, not the first
Are you to turn and ask thus. Sir, 'twas not
Her husband's presence only, called that spot
15 Of joy into the Duchess' cheek: perhaps
Frà Pandolf chanced to say 'Her mantle laps
Over my lady's wrist too much,' or 'Paint
Must never hope to reproduce the faint
Half-flush that dies along her throat': such stuff
20 Was courtesy, she thought, and cause enough
For calling up that spot of joy. She had
A heart – how shall I say? – too soon made glad,
Too easily impressed; she liked whate'er
She looked on, and her looks went everywhere.
25 Sir, 'twas all one! My favour at her breast,

Dramatic monologue – speaking to the count's representative

Duke's desire for control

'dies' and 'throat' **foreshadow** Duchess's death

Pronoun 'she' used throughout the poem – depersonalises Duchess who is never named

Repetition emphasises Duke's displeasure at Duchess's faults

Duke was not satisfied with his wife's opinions and behaviour

Exclamatory language and short sentence show strength of his feelings

16

MY LAST DUCHESS by Robert Browning

Dashes suggest his anger and incredulity

Juxtaposition of Duke's 'favour' and a lowly 'mule' suggests Duchess had no respect for rank or status

Status and power – respect for his status should outweigh all else

Irony – long monologue shows he does have this skill

Vocabulary highlights Duke's view of Duchess as an object

Verb suggests Duke's belief that she should have allowed him to control her behaviour

Tone is almost sarcastic, suggesting anger

Duke was not satisfied with his wife's opinions and behaviour

Juxtaposition – sudden change of subject suggests she was murdered, but it is of little importance

The dropping of the daylight in the West,
The bough of cherries some officious fool
Broke in the orchard for her, the white mule
She rode with round the terrace – all and each
30 Would draw from her alike the approving speech,
Or blush, at least. She thanked men, – good! But thanked
Somehow – I know not how – as if she ranked
My gift of a nine-hundred-years-old name
With anybody's gift. Who'd stoop to blame
35 This sort of trifling? Even had you skill
In speech – (which I have not) – to make your will
Quite clear to such an one, and say, 'Just this
Or that in you disgusts me; here you miss,
Or there exceed the mark' – and if she let
40 Herself be lessoned so, nor plainly set
Her wits to yours, forsooth, and made excuse,
– E'en then would be some stooping; and I choose
Never to stoop. Oh sir, she smiled, no doubt,
Whene'er I passed her; but who passed without
45 Much the same smile? This grew; I gave commands;
Then all smiles stopped together. There she stands
As if alive. Will't please you rise? We'll meet
The company below, then. I repeat,
The Count your master's known munificence
50 Is ample warrant that no just pretence
Of mine for dowry will be disallowed;
Though his fair daughter's self, as I avowed
At starting, is my object. Nay, we'll go
Together down, sir. Notice Neptune, though,
55 Taming a sea-horse, thought a rarity,
Which Claus of Innsbruck cast in bronze for me!

Attitude to women – he is arranging to marry his next Duchess

Ambiguity – murder is implied but not explicitly stated

Duke describes another of his possessions, suggesting he thinks his former wife, her painting and this statue are of similar worth

Final first **person pronoun** emphasises his self-centredness and arrogance

MY LAST DUCHESS by Robert Browning

What is the poem's setting?

- The poem is set in **sixteenth-century Italy**, in the house of the **Duke of Ferrara**.
- His house is decorated with **artworks** of which he is very **proud**; he boasts of Frà Pandolf's **skilled portrait** of the previous Duchess and the **'rarity'** of his bronze statue.

What is the poem about?

- The poem is written in the **voice** of the **Duke** of Ferrara as he describes a **portrait** of his **former wife**.
- The description of the **portrait** makes the Duke think about how **his wife disappointed** him by not appreciating **his attention** and **status**.
- It is suggested towards the end of the poem that the Duke **murdered** his wife.
- It is revealed that the Duke is **talking** to the representative of the Count whose **daughter he now hopes to marry**.
- The **theme** of **power** is implied in the fear with which the Duke is regarded (**'if they durst'**) and his ruthlessness in murdering his wife because he thought she was disrespectful.

Five key things about the language

1. The **possessive pronoun** in the title, 'My Last Duchess', suggests the Duke sees her as a possession.
2. The Duchess is never named, only referred to by the pronoun 'she', which effectively depersonalises her.
3. The Duke is the only speaker in this lengthy **dramatic monologue**, suggesting he does not allow interruption, but expects his listener's full attention. This impression is reinforced by the frequent use of enjambment.
4. The **repetition** of **'alive'** (ll. 2 and 47) draws attention to her death.
5. Browning uses features of spoken language, e.g. **exclamatory** phrases such as **'Oh sir'** and **direct address** (the pronoun **'you'**) to create this dramatic monologue.

Five key quotations

1. Duchess's flaws: 'she liked whate'er/She looked on, and her looks went everywhere' (ll. 23–4). The Duke suggests she should have reserved her appreciation only for him.

2. Expectations of respect: 'as if she ranked/My gift of a nine-hundred-years-old name/With anybody's gift.' (ll. 32–4). The **verb** 'ranked' has **connotations** of hierarchy.

3. Enjoyment of nature: 'The dropping of the daylight in the West,/ ... the white mule' (ll. 26–8). The Duke lists all the pleasures that the Duchess should not have valued.

4. Arrogance: 'and I choose/Never to stoop' (ll. 42–3). Enjambment positions 'Never' at the beginning of the line for emphasis.

5. **Ambiguity**: 'all smiles stopped together' (l. 46). The short phrase implies suddenness. Was she killed?

Note it!

Compare Browning's presentation of the Duke's expectations of his wife with the expectations explored in 'Kamikaze'. Do the poets create sympathy for these figures in a similar way?

Exam focus

How can I write about Browning's use of voice? AO2

You can explore how the Duke's voice suggests his power and status.

Browning creates the voice of the Duke through language choices that imply his arrogant view of his status. For example, the verb 'stoop' implies lowering his rank and he emphatically declares 'I choose/Never to stoop'. Instead, he chooses to murder his wife, suggesting how ruthlessly he punishes those who do not respect his position in society.

- Makes clear point about the theme
- Quotations carefully selected
- Develops analysis further

Now you try!

Finish this paragraph about another theme. Use one of the quotations from the list.

The Duke makes clear the ways in which his wife failed to meet his expectations of respect. For example, ...

THE CHARGE OF THE LIGHT BRIGADE
by Alfred, Lord Tennyson

This poem describes a charge made by the British army during the Crimean War (1853–6). The brigade's commanders made a tactical error due to miscommunication. More than two-thirds of the brigade were killed or wounded. The poem, which celebrates the men's bravery in unquestioningly obeying orders, was published six weeks after the charge.

1.

1 Half a league, half a league,
Half a league onward,
All in the valley of Death
   Rode the six hundred.
5 'Forward, the Light Brigade!
Charge for the guns!' he said:
Into the valley of Death
   Rode the six hundred.

2.

'Forward, the Light Brigade!'
10 Was there a man dismay'd?
Not tho' the soldier knew
   Some one had blunder'd:
Theirs not to make reply,
Theirs not to reason why,
15 Theirs but to do and die:
Into the valley of Death
   Rode the six hundred.

3.

Cannon to right of them,
Cannon to left of them,
20 Cannon in front of them
   Volley'd and thunder'd;
Storm'd at with shot and shell,
Boldly they rode and well,
Into the jaws of Death,
25 Into the mouth of Hell
   Rode the six hundred.

Use of **dialogue** suggests narrator was an eyewitness, implying an accurate account

Strong repetition, **rhythm** and **rhyme** make poem memorable

Allusion to Psalm 23 highlights deadly nature of the conflict

Rhetorical question implies soldiers' courage

Repetition emphasises soldiers' sense of duty and bravery

Power and status: soldiers have no choice but to follow orders

Repetition shows how soldiers are surrounded by danger

Metaphorical verb suggests violence of cannon blasts

Alliteration relays sounds of battle

Near-**synonyms** create an image of the battle devouring the soldiers – repeated in stanza 5 to emphasise their heroism

4.

Flash'd all their sabres bare,
Flash'd as they turn'd in air
Sabring the gunners there,
30 Charging an army, while
 All the world wonder'd:
Plunged in the battery-smoke
Right thro' the line they broke;
Cossack and Russian
35 Reel'd from the sabre-stroke
 Shatter'd and sunder'd.
Then they rode back, but not
 Not the six hundred.

5.

Cannon to right of them,
40 Cannon to left of them,
Cannon behind them
 Volley'd and thunder'd;
Storm'd at with shot and shell,
While horse and hero fell,
45 They that had fought so well
Came thro' the jaws of Death
Back from the mouth of Hell,
All that was left of them,
 Left of six hundred.

6.

50 When can their glory fade?
O the wild charge they made!
 All the world wonder'd.
Honour the charge they made!
Honour the Light Brigade,
55 Noble six hundred!

Imagery of sight as well as sound

Violent-sounding **verbs** highlight soldiers' bravery

Attitudes to war: suggests soldiers' bravery and physicality of battle

Repetition across the line break creates a dramatic pause, slowing the pace as outcome of charge is revealed

Parallels to **stanza** 3 show soldiers' return

'imagery' Natural imagery conveys violence of the battle

Dactylic dimeter replicates sound of horses' galloping hooves

Repetition of 'left' emphasises the huge loss of men

Repetition of line highlights the wondrous bravery of the soldiers: they deserve to be wondered at

Imperative verb directs audience's response

The only time an **adjective** is attached to this repeated phrase: the final, lasting impression of these soldiers

THE CHARGE OF THE LIGHT BRIGADE by Alfred, Lord Tennyson

What is the poem's setting?

- The poem describes the **charge into battle** of six hundred men on horseback.
- The poet vividly conveys the **sights, sounds, danger** and **chaos** of the **battlefield**.

What is the poem about?

- Six hundred soldiers charge directly towards the **Russian guns**, during the Battle of Balaclava.
- The soldiers know that a **mistake has been made** but they **do not question their orders** to charge.
- They meet the enemy in a valley. The **soldiers fight bravely** but **many are killed or wounded**.
- The **theme** of **power** is evident in the soldiers' **unquestioning obedience**, and **conflict** in the **violence** of battle.
- The poet calls for all to **celebrate the soldiers' bravery**.

Five key things about the language

1. Tennyson uses **repetition** throughout the poem to convey the danger of the conflict, and the bravery of the soldiers. In conjunction with the relentless **rhythm**, it evokes the pace of the charge.
2. He uses **figurative language** to convey the violence of battle: **'thunder'd'**, **'Storm'd'**, **'jaws of Death'**.
3. Positive **adverbs** focus the reader's attention on the soldiers' achievement (**'Boldly'**, **'well'**) rather than their commanding officers' error.
4. Tennyson selects **emotive verbs** (**'Flash'd'**, **'Plunged'**, **'Reel'd'**) to convey the dramatic action.
5. He uses **imperative verbs** to direct the reader's response.

22

Five key quotations

1. Inevitable death: 'the valley of Death' (l. 3). A dramatic and **emotive** reference to the battlefield, implying the consequences of the charge were inevitably deadly.
2. Dramatic language: 'thunder'd ... Storm'd ... Charging ... Plunged' (ll. 21–32). Verb choices suggest the chaotic action and pace of the battle.
3. Danger: 'Cannon to right of them,/Cannon to left of them' (ll. 39–40). The repetitive structure highlights the danger into which the soldiers were ordered to charge.
4. Heroism: 'horse and hero fell' (l. 44). **Alliteration** links the death of soldiers and their horses, creating sympathy for both.
5. Reader's response: 'Honour the Light Brigade,/Noble six hundred!' (ll. 54–5). Tennyson clearly directs the reader to respect the soldiers' bravery.

Note it!

Compare Tennyson's depiction of war with that of Hughes' in 'Bayonet Charge'. Do they express a similar **viewpoint**?

Exam focus

How can I write about Tennyson's use of language? AO2

You can analyse Tennyson's viewpoint to explore his depiction of war.

> The language choices in the poem present the battle as chaotic and dramatic. For example, the verbs 'thunder'd' and 'Storm'd' use sounds taken from nature to convey the cannon fire while 'Charging' and 'Plunged' create a sense of frantic action, helping to focus the reader on the bravery of the soldiers. However, although praising their bravery, the poet also briefly mentions that 'Some one had blunder'd', suggesting that he blames their deaths on this mistake.

- Topic sentence makes clear point
- Carefully chosen words
- Signals a development of the analysis
- Explores different parts of the poem

Now you try!

Finish this paragraph about another theme. Use one of the quotations from the list.

The poet strongly suggests how he feels the reader should respond to the deaths of the soldiers. He does this through ....

EXPOSURE by Wilfred Owen

Wilfred Owen fought and died in the First World War (1914–18). In 1916, Owen was sent to hospital suffering from the effects of war. This poem was written in 1918, when he had returned to the Front. It explores the soldiers' suffering due to the conditions in which they were trying to survive.

Shows this isn't just one individual's opinion or experience

Refrain-like repetition emphasises monotony of soldiers' experience

Half-rhymes create disharmony, suggesting tension

Present **tense** creates immediacy: the reader shares the soldiers' experience as it happens

Ellipses convey idea of endless emptiness

1 Our brains ache, in the merciless iced east winds that knive us ...
Wearied we keep awake because the night is silent ...
Low, drooping flares confuse our memory of the salient ...
Worried by silence, sentries whisper, curious, nervous,
5   But nothing happens.

Watching, we hear the mad gusts tugging on the wire,
Like twitching agonies of men among its brambles.
Northward, incessantly, the flickering gunnery rumbles,
Far off, like a dull rumour of some other war.
10   What are we doing here?

The poignant misery of dawn begins to grow ...
We only know war lasts, rain soaks, and clouds sag stormy.
Dawn massing in the east her melancholy army
Attacks once more in ranks on shivering ranks of grey,
15   But nothing happens.

Sudden successive flights of bullets streak the silence.
Less deadly than the air that shudders black with snow,
With sidelong flowing flakes that flock, pause, and renew,
We watch them wandering up and down the wind's nonchalance,
20   But nothing happens.

Soldiers are detached from the fighting

Rhetorical question conveys sense of uncertainty and purposelessness

Repetition of **conjunction** emphasises that, whatever changes in soldiers' experience, still nothing happens

Nature seems more deadly than war

Personification of weather connects it to beleaguered army

Personification presents the wind as indifferent and detached

Nature is threatening

Movement of time from winter to spring – but no change in soldiers' experiences

Personification presents snow as sinister and invasive

Unusual **compound adjectives** summarise and emphasise effect of weather

Repetition of 'dying' in final line of this stanza and next two **stanzas**: death of hope fills soldiers' minds

Pale flakes with fingering stealth come feeling for our faces –
We cringe in holes, back on forgotten dreams, and stare, snow-dazed,
Deep into grassier ditches. So we drowse, sun-dozed,
Littered with blossoms trickling where the blackbird fusses.
25   – Is it that we are dying?

Slowly our ghosts drag home: glimpsing the sunk fires, glozed
With crusted dark-red jewels; crickets jingle there;
For hours the innocent mice rejoice: the house is theirs;
Shutters and doors, all closed: on us the doors are closed, –
30   We turn back to our dying.

Repetition contrasts experiences of warm mice and cold soldiers

Since we believe not otherwise can kind fires burn;
Now ever suns smile true on child, or field, or fruit.
For God's invincible spring our love is made afraid;
Therefore, not loath, we lie out here; therefore were born,
35   For love of God seems dying.

Complex expression suggests confused feelings about the purpose of war

Tonight, His frost will fasten on this mud and us,
Shrivelling many hands, puckering foreheads crisp.
The burying-party, picks and shovels in their shaking grasp,
Pause over half-known faces. All their eyes are ice,
40   But nothing happens.

The loss of hope and faith in God

Metaphor conveys absence of emotion in soldiers' hardened attitudes to death

Soldiers and mud have become indistinguishable

EXPOSURE by Wilfred Owen

What is the poem's setting?

- The poem is set in the **trenches in France** during the **First World War**.
- It is a **harsh, unforgiving environment** of **'winds'**, **'rain'**, **'snow'** and **'mud'**.

What is the poem about?

- The poem describes the **experiences** of a group of **soldiers**.
- The soldiers feel **detached** from the war as they **wait** in their trenches, listening for any sound that suggests they may be called upon to fight.

- They occasionally see bullets but feel more **under attack** from the **weather**.
- Frost settles on them at night. Some **die**. Still the soldiers are **not called upon** to fight.
- The **theme** of **conflict** is evident in the poem's setting of the First World War trenches, but also in the **aggressive depiction of nature**, and in the **speaker's mood**.

Five key things about the language

1. **Repetition** in the **refrain**-like final line of each **stanza** conveys the soldiers' frustration, powerlessness and loss of hope.
2. Owen uses **personification** and **emotive** language (**'the merciless iced east winds that knive us'**) to convey the threat of nature.
3. **Rhetorical questions** create a **tone** of uncertainty and fear (**'Is it that we are dying?'**).
4. Owen uses a **semantic field** related to suffering to highlight the soldiers' experience: **'agonies'**, **'misery'**, **'shudders'**.
5. The deadly frost described in the final stanza is attributed to God: **'Tonight, His frost'**, reflecting the **viewpoint** that the soldiers' **'love of God seems dying'**.

Five key quotations

1. Threat of nature: **'the merciless iced east winds that knive us'** (l. 1). The **verb** 'knive' personifies the weather, suggesting its deadly aggression.

2. Powerlessness: **'But nothing happens.'** (ll. 5, 15, 20, 40). Repetition suggests frustration and fear.

3. Injustice and powerlessness: **'the innocent mice rejoice'** (l. 28). The image of mice in a warm house highlights the soldiers' sense of injustice and dissatisfaction.

4. Loss of hope: **'love of God seems dying'** (l. 35). The soldiers feel their situation is hopeless and that even God has forsaken them.

5. Emotional coldness: **'their eyes are ice'** (l. 39). The soldiers' emotions are frozen as they watch their comrades die.

Note it!

Compare the experience of war shown in 'Exposure' with Tennyson's presentation of it in 'The Charge of the Light Brigade'. What differences are there in the response that each poet is trying to create in the reader?

Exam focus

How can I write about Owen's use of repetition? (AO2)

You can explore how Owen uses repetition to express his attitude to war.

Owen uses repetition to emphasise his negative thoughts and feelings. For example, the final line 'But nothing happens' concludes four of the poem's eight stanzas, creating an impression of overpowering frustration and powerlessness. Moreover, the repetition of 'dying' in three of these final lines suggests that death is constantly in the poet's mind, conveying the loss of all hope.	Makes clear point about Owen's attitude to war
	Carefully chosen evidence
	Signals a developed analysis
	Explores key technique in more depth

Now you try!

Finish this paragraph about another theme. Use one of the quotations from the list.

The poet focuses on the threat of nature and the soldiers' environment much more closely than the dangers of warfare. This is suggested in ....

STORM ON THE ISLAND by Seamus Heaney

This poem was written at the start of 'The Troubles' in Northern Ireland, where the main government building is called Stormont. It could be read as a political allegory which touches on outbreaks of violence.

Wind's strength emphasised by **enjambment** and **alliteration**

Nature **personified** as potentially friendly

Ironic tone implies hay would be a problem if it were to grow

Use of 'we' creates sense of community; present **tense** creates immediacy

Conversational tone

1 We are prepared: we build our houses squat,
   Sink walls in rock and roof them with good slate.
   The wizened earth had never troubled us
   With hay, so, as you see, there are no stacks
5 Or stooks that can be lost. Nor are there trees
   Which might prove company when it blows full
   Blast: you know what I mean – leaves and branches
   Can raise a tragic chorus in a gale
   So that you can listen to the thing you fear
10 Forgetting that it pummels your house too.
   But there are no trees, no natural shelter.
   You might think that the sea is company,
   Exploding comfortably down on the cliffs
   But no: when it begins, the flung spray hits
15 The very windows, spits like a tame cat
   Turned savage. We just sit tight while wind dives
   And strafes invisibly. Space is a salvo.
   We are bombarded by the empty air.
   Strange, it is a huge nothing that we fear.

Personification of gale links to dramatic chorus in tragic drama who warned audience or commented on events

We can become seduced by drama, forgetting how dangerous the reality is

Repetition of key words from earlier reinforces idea of nature seeming safe (though it isn't)

Simile evokes sense of something once trusted becoming unpredictable and violent

Wind, which can do harm, is not a physical thing. What implications might this have allegorically or symbolically?

Semantic field is militaristic, linking to violent conflict in Ireland

Blank verse with irregular enjambment and **caesurae** mimics natural speech

28

What is the poem's setting?

- The poem refers to **isolated cottages** on **Ireland's exposed coastline**.
- It is a **harsh environment** with **'wizened'** earth, suggesting the soil is like the skin of an old person or creature.

What is the poem about?

- Heaney describes the island's **stormy weather** but the **violent imagery** suggests this reflects Ireland's **troubled history**.

- The **theme** of **power** is explored in the strength of conflict between the storm and the buildings, e.g. the speaker describes how the community's houses are built to withstand stormy weather.
- However, the landscape is wide open so **buildings are isolated** with nothing to deflect the wind or storms.
- The **sea** is also aggressive and **'savage'**, which adds to the sense of a **vulnerable place**.
- Finally, the speaker **compares the wind and air to gunfire**, but also suggests it is like the vacuum created by an explosion, reminding the reader of the **political context**.

Five key things about the language

1. Heaney uses the plural **personal** and **possessive pronouns** **'we'** and **'our'** to create a **viewpoint** which is that of the whole community, as if explaining their world to outsiders.
2. **Figurative language** in the form of personification, similes and **metaphors** conveys the power of the storm and sea.
3. Heaney uses a conversational, informal **tone** from time to time through **direct address** (**'you know what I mean'**) and **colloquial** phrases (**'as you see'**) as if to convey an untroubled, everyday **mood** – at odds with the reality of the situation.
4. He uses the semantic field of attack and warfare which increases in strength as the poem progresses.
5. His use of violent imagery and the play on the word 'Stormont' – '**Storm on the Island**' – links the natural conflict to real division between people.

Five key quotations

1. Used to harsh weather: **'We are prepared'** (l. 1). The Irish have learned to live in this difficult environment.

2. Power of weather: **'it pummels your house'** (l. 10). The **verb** 'pummels' suggests a continuous thumping or hitting.

3. Sound of the storm: **'a tragic chorus in a gale'** (l. 8). The metaphor of the chorus links to the tragedy of the Irish situation at the time, in which so many had lost their lives or suffered.

4. Isolation: **'no trees, no natural shelter'** (l. 11). The **repetition** of 'no' emphasises the exposure to the elements.

5. Unexpected conflict: **'spits like a tame cat/Turned savage'** (ll. 15–16). The **simile** suggests how everyday domestic things can conceal violence and savagery.

Note it!

Compare Heaney's view of the savage power of nature with Wordsworth's feelings of awe when looking at the mountain peak in 'Extract from The Prelude'. Are they the same feelings?

Exam focus

How can I write about the theme of nature's power?

You can analyse the **semantic field** used by Heaney to explore its power.

> Heaney's use of a range of verbs related to violent warfare intensifies the presentation of nature's force. For example, words such as 'Exploding', 'strafes' and 'bombarded' suggest the wind is attacking the coastline mercilessly. However, this use of militaristic terms also reflects the political context of Ireland at the time when Heaney was writing, which was one of British army occupation and a form of civil war.

- Topic sentence makes clear point
- Carefully chosen words
- Signals an alternative interpretation
- Knowledge of wider context

Now you try!

Finish this paragraph about another theme. Use one of the quotations from the list.

The poet also suggests that the Irish are used to the harsh weather. This is highlighted in ....

My progress   Needs more work ☐   Getting there ☐   Sorted! ☐

SPECIAL FOCUS 3: Mood and tone

What are mood and tone?

- The **mood** or **tone** of a poem is the **atmosphere** or **feeling evoked**.

How do I identify these in a poem like 'Storm on the Island'?

- Explore the **connotations** of **particular words** or **phrases**, e.g. **'savage'** suggests extreme brutality and uncivilised violence.
- Think about how **particular vocabulary is linked**, e.g. all the words related to warfare or the military – **'Exploding'**, **'strafes'**, **'bombarded'**, etc.
- Consider the **voice** of the speaker or 'narrator' of the poem – their **viewpoint** or **attitude**, e.g. the use of **'we'** to suggest community, or **modal verbs** to suggest thoughtfulness – **'You *might* think'**.
- Think about the **sound**, **pace** and **rhythm**, e.g. is the poem structured to create a fast pace, or a slower, more reflective pace?
- Look for **change** or **development** in the mood or tone, e.g. in how the reader might respond to the increasingly violent **imagery** in the poem.

Exam focus

How can I write about mood and tone?

You could use **adjectives** or **adverbs** related to viewpoint or language, e.g. *reflective, generally thoughtful, increasingly violent.*

While conflict is at the heart of the poem, the tone is reflective with the use of modal verbs such as 'might' to suggest a thoughtful evaluation of the situation. Even the opening 'We are prepared' suggests a careful way of looking at the violence. However, by the end of the poem the poet doesn't seem to have the answers, so the mood changes to a slightly fearful one.	Evidence from the language
	Mood adjectives/adverbs
	How tone/mood develops

Now you try!

Think about the other poems in the cluster. Do any of them share a similar thoughtful, reflective tone?

BAYONET CHARGE by Ted Hughes

This poem describes a bayonet charge: when soldiers run towards the enemy with a bayonet (a kind of knife) fixed to the barrel of their guns. This was a common method of attack in the First World War. The poem is focused on the experience of one soldier.

Surprising **verb** choice conveys difficulty and confusion

Metaphor evokes physical violence

Alliteration adds emphasis and highlights **rhythm** of the running

Sensory **imagery** creates sense of soldier's physical experience

Three **stanzas** break action into three acts: running, stillness, running

Simile suggests heat and extreme pain: horrific reality of war that eclipses heroic feelings

Metaphor suggests his lack of control: his nation and the stars control his fate

Soldier is unaware of why he is doing what he is doing, or why he is there

Simile suggests soldier's stillness: a moment, frozen in time

1 Suddenly he awoke and was running – raw
In raw-seamed hot khaki, his sweat heavy,
Stumbling across a field of clods towards a green hedge
That dazzled with rifle fire, hearing
5 Bullets smacking the belly out of the air –
He lugged a rifle numb as a smashed arm;
The patriotic tear that had brimmed in his eye
Sweating like molten iron from the centre of his chest, –

In bewilderment then he almost stopped –
10 In what cold clockwork of the stars and the nations
Was he the hand pointing that second? He was running
Like a man who has jumped up in the dark and runs
Listening between his footfalls for the reason
Of his still running, and his foot hung like
15 Statuary in mid-stride. Then the shot-slashed furrows

Threw up a yellow hare that rolled like a flame
And crawled in a threshing circle, its mouth wide
Open silent, its eyes standing out.
He plunged past with his bayonet toward the green hedge,
20 King, honour, human dignity, etcetera
Dropped like luxuries in a yelling alarm
To get out of that blue crackling air
His terror's touchy dynamite.

Uneven rhythm, line length and enjambment echo soldier's panicked and haphazard thoughts and movement

List of typical war poetry **themes**: ideals considered worth fighting for, but belittled by final word 'etcetera'

Image of terrified hare a metaphor for suffering of soldiers?

What is the poem's setting?

- The poem describes a **soldier** in a **conflict** that is unnamed, but likely to be the First World War.

- The reference to an **everyday image** of a green hedge, rather than the enemy who are apparently firing from behind it, implies the soldier's **uncertainty of his motives** in fighting.

What is the poem about?

- A soldier **charges through rifle fire** towards the enemy, with his bayonet fixed.

- The soldier stops in mid-charge: **unsure** of why he is running; questioning the purpose of war.

- He sees a **hare** on the battle field. It is **dying**.

- The sight of the hare shocks the soldier into **charging** again, apparently **running in panic** to escape the rifle fire.

- The **theme of powerlessness** in war is explored: he does not understand what he is doing, or why; he is just a part of the **'cold clockwork of the stars and the nations'** that control his life and death.

Five key things about the language

1. Hughes uses vivid vocabulary to evoke the sights and sounds of battle, e.g. **'dazzled', smacking', 'yelling'**.

2. **Figurative language** conveys the physical pain of war: **'raw-seamed hot khaki', 'Sweating like molten iron'**.

3. Alliteration highlights the fear and violence of war: **'shot-slashed', 'plunged past'**.

4. The image of a dying hare is vividly conveyed through simile and dramatic verbs: **'Threw up', 'rolled', 'crawled', 'threshing'**.

5. Hughes **juxtaposes** the ideals of **'King, honour, human dignity'** with **'a yelling alarm/To get out of that blue crackling air'**. Fear and the desperate urge to survive completely override the **'luxuries'** of these ideals.

Five key quotations

1. Physical experience: 'raw/In raw-seamed hot khaki' (ll. 1–2). The **adjective** 'raw' implies vulnerability and pain.

2. Brutality: 'He lugged a rifle numb as a smashed arm' (l. 6). The use of violent language suggests the pain and misery of war.

3. Confusion: 'In bewilderment then he almost stopped' (l. 9). The **noun** 'bewilderment' has **connotations** of both confusion and disorientation.

4. Frozen: 'in mid-stride' (l. 15). This **prepositional phrase** conveys the image of the soldier's movement interrupted, frozen in his confusion.

5. Survival: 'To get out of that blue crackling air' (l. 22). The **verb** 'get out' bluntly expresses the desire to escape; the sight, sound and terrors of battle.

Note it!

Compare the experience of the soldier depicted in 'Bayonet Charge' with that of the soldiers in 'Exposure'. What does each suggest about the poet's attitude to war?

Exam focus

How can I write about the theme of the effects of war?

You can explore Hughes's use of **imagery** to analyse his **viewpoint** on the effects of war.

Hughes vividly depicts a soldier frozen in confusion in the middle of a battle. He uses a simile to compare him to a man who has jumped up in the dark'. The verb 'jumped' implies shock while the adverbial 'in the dark' suggests lack of understanding. Hughes develops this simile later in the stanza where repetition of 'running' in this long, multiclause sentence powerfully reflects the sense of 'bewilderment'.

Makes clear point about the effects of war

Short, relevant quotation

Signals further analysis

Develops the language analysis

Now you try!

Finish this paragraph about another **theme**. Use one of the quotations from the list.

The poet's use of violent language in the first part of the poem conveys the brutality of the conflict. For example, ...

My progress Needs more work ☐ Getting there ☐ Sorted! ☐

What do I need to do?

- You need to refer to **words**, **phrases**, **lines** or **verses/stanzas** from the poem in a clear way which enables you to **explain** or **interpret** ideas.

How do I do it?

- Refer clearly to the **specific position** of your reference, e.g. *in the second verse, the final line*.
- Select the **most appropriate** and **relevant** quotation or reference.
- **Only quote** or **refer to** what you **definitely need** (don't quote several lines at a time).
- Make sure **direct quotations** are placed in **speech marks**; or if you **paraphrase**, use your **own words**.
- **Embed** any quotations **fluently** in your statements, e.g. *The poet describes the soldier as 'raw/In raw-seamed hot khaki', which suggests his discomfort and vulnerability.*
- **Explain** meaning, but also **interpret** or **infer** (**suggest** wider **connections** or **ideas**).

Exam focus

How can I use quotations and references effectively?

Look at this example in which a student comments on Hughes's presentation of war in 'Bayonet Charge'.

> Hughes presents war as a terrifying and confusing experience. In the second stanza, as the soldier charges across the battlefield, he pauses 'In bewilderment', showing his feelings of confusion, but also implying his fear and disorientation.

- Identifies the position of the reference
- Paraphrases to put quotation in context
- Short, focused, relevant embedded quotation
- Explains meaning
- Infers/interprets feelings

Now you try!

Use the quotation 'To get out of that blue crackling air' to write a paragraph about the presentation of war in 'Bayonet Charge'.

My progress   Needs more work ☐   Getting there ☐   Sorted! ☐   **35**

REMAINS by Simon Armitage

This poem explores the impact of war on those who fight. It is taken from a collection of poems by Armitage, published under the title 'The Not Dead', for which he interviewed many soldiers who had fought in war zones in the Middle East.

Conversational language suggests a story being told

Colloquial language throughout helps to create the **voice** of the soldier

Effects of war: the title suggests both the physical remains of the dead man and the lasting psychological impact of the experience on the soldier

1   On another occasion, we get sent out
    to tackle looters raiding a bank.
    And one of them legs it up the road,
    probably armed, possibly not.

No one is named here, for anonymity or because it is significant only that soldiers are opening fire

5   Well myself and somebody else and somebody else
    are all of the same mind,
    so all three of us open fire.
    Three of a kind all letting fly, and I swear

Everyday language is a **euphemism** for the man's disembowelment. Is the speaker reluctant to face up to what he has done?

    I see every round as it rips through his life –
10 I see broad daylight on the other side.
    So we've hit this looter a dozen times
    and he's there on the ground, sort of inside out,

    pain itself, the image of agony.
    One of my mates goes by

Casual **verbs** imply desensitisation to violence

15 and tosses his guts back into his body.
    Then he's carted off in the back of a lorry.

    End of story, except not really.
    His blood-shadow stays on the street, and out on patrol
    I walk right over it week after week.
20 Then I'm home on leave. But I blink

Irony: the event is finished but its impact is not

Metaphor implying the blood stain on the street, and on the soldier's memory. The noun 'shadow' has connotations of darkness and fear

36

Irregular rhythm and informal sentence structure suggests conversational speech

Enjambment between stanzas, suggests the memories are unstoppable

and he bursts again through the doors of the bank.
Sleep, and he's probably armed, possibly not.
Dream, and he's torn apart by a dozen rounds.
And the drink and the drugs won't flush him out –

Memory: nothing will eradicate this memory

25 he's here in my head when I close my eyes,
dug in behind enemy lines,
not left for dead in some distant, sun-stunned, sand-smothered land
or six-feet-under in desert sand,

but near to the knuckle, here and now,
30 his bloody life in my bloody hands.

Final short **stanza** gives emphasis to the poem's key focus: the constant re-living of horrific memories of killing

Used **ambiguously** as a curse and a descriptive **adjective**. **Repetition** links man's death and soldier's anger

Idiom suggests it's hard to bear

Sibilance and **half-rhyme** ('stunned'/'land') make this jarring and awkward, like the memories it conjures

The tormenting power of a single moment

REMAINS by Simon Armitage

What is the poem's setting?

- The poem relates the story of a **soldier killing a looter** in a **Middle Eastern war zone**, the memory of which haunts him when out on patrol.
- Even when home on leave, he is **haunted by the memory** from that **'sun-stunned, sand-smothered land'**.

What is the poem about?

- Told in the **voice** of a soldier, the poem describes the **killing of a looter** in **disturbing detail**.
- At first the soldier seems **untroubled** by the death, casually describing how his comrade **'tosses his guts back into his body'**.
- However, weeks later, **on patrol**, the soldier is **still aware** of the dead man's **'blood-shadow'** on the street.
- Even when home on leave, the soldier cannot **'flush ... out'** the memory with drink and drugs, suggesting a deterioration in his mental health.
- The **themes** of **conflict** and the **effects of war** are explored in the **troubled mind** of the soldier.

Five key things about the language

1. **Colloquial** language creates a conversational **tone** as the soldier first recounts his story.
2. The use of **imagery** and **figurative language** then conveys the soldier's trouble memories after the incident, e.g. the **metaphor 'blood-shadow'** and the image of the looter **'dug in behind enemy lines'** – i.e. dug into the soldier's mind.
3. Throughout, vocabulary from the **semantic fields** of battle and violence (**'armed'**, **'open fire'**, **'rips'**, **'torn apart'**, **'bloody'**) highlights and links the violence of the incident and the violence of the soldier's memories.
4. The title links the human remains of the looter, the soldier's memories and their destructive impact upon him.
5. **Repetition** and **alliteration** (**'near ... knuckle'**) give the short final stanza dramatic emphasis, summarising the soldier's suffering.

Five key quotations

1. Violence: 'I see every round as it rips through his life' (l. 9). The **verb** 'rips' suggests destruction.

2. Casual attitude: 'he's carted off in the back of a lorry' (l. 16). **Colloquial** verb 'carted' implies the soldier is unaffected by war.

3. Effects of war: 'His blood-shadow stays on the street' (l. 18). This metaphor has **connotations** of violence, darkness and overshadowing.

4. Memory: 'Dream, and he's torn apart by a dozen rounds' (l. 23). Informal sentence structure suggests the soldier's disturbed sleep.

5. Lasting effects: 'here and now,/his bloody life in my bloody hands' (ll. 29–30). The repeated **adjective** 'bloody' conveys the soldier's continuing guilt and anger.

Note it!

Compare Armitage's depiction of the impact of war with Hughes's in 'Bayonet Charge'. The setting and focus of the poems are different but is there any similarity in the thoughts and feelings of the soldiers described?

Exam focus

How can I write about the theme of the effects of war?

You can explore Armitage's vocabulary choices to suggest the effects of war on the soldier.

> In the voice of the soldier, Armitage describes memories of the killing using violent language. For example, 'bursts' and 'torn apart' suggest the vividness and violence of the memories that haunt the soldier. These choices echo the vocabulary used to describe the original incident, suggesting that the violence of the killing has not faded even though time has passed.

Topic sentence makes clear point
Carefully chosen words support the point being made
Signals a link with another part of the poem
Explores the cumulative effect of the poet's choices

Now you try!

Finish this paragraph about another theme. Use one of the quotations from the list.

The poet also suggests the soldier's feelings of guilt and anger prompted by these memories. This is explored in ....

POPPIES by Jane Weir

This poem explores the feelings of a mother remembering when she said goodbye to her son. Although it is not explicitly stated, it may be implied that the son has left to join the army. The poem is filled with references to war and to death, suggesting the mother's fears.

Loose structure of 6-, 11- and 12-line **stanzas**; lines of around 10 syllables; creates a sense of control and of natural speech

1   Three days before Armistice Sunday
and poppies had already been placed
on individual war graves. Before you left,
I pinned one onto your lapel, crimped petals,
5   spasms of paper red, disrupting a blockade
of yellow bias binding around your blazer.

Sellotape bandaged around my hand,
I rounded up as many white cat hairs
as I could, smoothed down your shirt's
10   upturned collar, steeled the softening
of my face. I wanted to graze my nose
across the tip of your nose, play at
being Eskimos like we did when
you were little. I resisted the impulse
15   to run my fingers through the gelled
blackthorns of your hair. All my words
flattened, rolled, turned into felt,

Remembrance: references to Armistice Sunday imply thoughts of death in war

Language of pain; **imagery** suggesting blood

Language from a military **semantic field**

Strong contrast to all the fabric imagery, implying strength, a hardening of emotions

Memories: the son's childhood brought back by thoughts of loss

Metaphor could imply a release of emotion, or releasing her son into the adult world

Enjambment positions this phrase at start of line for emphasis: the impact of her son's departure

Simile implies possibility: is this the son's perception of a world of possibilities in the army?

> slowly melting. I was brave, as I walked
> with you, to the front door, threw
> 20 it open, the world overflowing
> like a treasure chest. A split second
> and you were away, intoxicated.
> After you'd gone I went into your bedroom,
> released a song bird from its cage.
> 25 Later a single dove flew from the pear tree,
> and this is where it has led me,
> skirting the church yard walls, my stomach busy
> making tucks, darts, pleats, hat-less, without
> a winter coat or reinforcements of scarf, gloves.
>
> 30 On reaching the top of the hill I traced
> the inscriptions on the war memorial,
> leaned against it like a wishbone.
> The dove pulled freely against the sky,
> an ornamental stitch. I listened, hoping to hear
> 35 your playground voice catching on the wind.

Time markers used throughout the poem to manage complex time shifts

Metaphor conveys anxiety through clothing-related imagery

Ambiguity: is her son's name inscribed on the memorial? Or is she connecting her fears for her son with others who have died?

Simile could imply she's making a wish

Metaphor linking **images** of textiles and peace; linking feelings of tension and longing for peace

Innocence: implies memories of son's childhood could bring some comfort

41

POPPIES by Jane Weir

What is the poem's setting?

- A **mother** says **goodbye** to her **son**, seeing him out of the front door, then goes upstairs to his bedroom.
- She climbs a hill to a **war memorial**, implying thoughts of **war** and **death**.

What is the poem about?

- A **mother remembers saying goodbye** to her son as he leaves home. It may be implied that he has joined the **army** and, perhaps, has **died**.

- She smartens him up before he leaves, pinning a **poppy** on to his jacket, removing cat hairs from it, smoothing his collar.
- The **son leaves** and his mother goes to his bedroom where it is implied she releases her emotions, and perhaps, **metaphorically**, her son too.
- She climbs a hill to a **war memorial** and traces the names of those who have fallen in battle. It is **unclear** if her son's name is inscribed there.
- **Conflict** is explored in the mother's thoughts as her son leaves home, perhaps to join the army.

Five key things about the language

1. The **themes** of war, death and commemoration are implied through references to Armistice Sunday, poppies, graves and a war memorial.
2. The sense of touch, and references to texture, evoke memories of events: **'Sellotape bandaged'**, **'the gelled/blackthorns of your hair'**.
3. The poem uses the first **person** and **direct address** to create a strong sense of the mother's **voice** and her relationship with her son.
4. The son's feelings of hope, possibility and excitement are implied in the **simile 'the world overflowing/like a treasure chest'** and the **adjective 'intoxicated'**.
5. Complex **images** of release, freedom and peace are conveyed through bird metaphors: a song bird is released from its cage; a dove, symbol of peace, flies.

Five key quotations

1. **Anxiety:** 'my stomach busy/making tucks, darts, pleats' (ll. 27–8). Imagery of a stomach sewn in complex folds suggests feelings of anxiety.

2. **Images of war and death:** 'poppies had already been placed/on individual war graves' (ll. 2–3). Imagery implies significance of war and death from the very beginning of the poem.

3. **Freedom:** 'I went into your bedroom,/released a song bird from its cage' (l. 23–4). This image of freedom echoes the moment the mother 'threw' the door open, releasing her son into the world.

4. **Vulnerability:** 'without/a winter coat or reinforcements of scarf, gloves' (ll. 28–9). Implies the mother's fragility following the loss of her son.

5. **Hope:** 'hoping to hear/your playground voice catching on the wind' (ll. 34–5). Memories of a childhood, now ended.

Note it!

Compare Weir's exploration of the power of memory with Armitage's in 'Remains'. Are similar ideas expressed in a similar way?

Exam focus

How can I write about the theme of memory? (AO1)

You can analyse Weir's use of imagery evoking childhood to explore her presentation of memory.

> Weir creates a strong sense of the mother's memories of her son's childhood. For example, the mother describes resisting the temptation to 'play at/being Eskimos like we did when/you were little'. The word 'play' evokes childhood, while the temptation suggests that her affection for him has not changed, though he is now grown up. However, it is unclear whether these memories are prompted by him leaving her, or if he has died in battle.

Topic sentence makes clear point about the theme of memory

Carefully chosen evidence supports the point being made

Signals a development in the analysis

Explores an ambiguity

Now you try!

Finish this paragraph about another theme. Use one of the quotations from the list.

The poet also suggests that the mother has allowed her son his freedom in leaving her. This is implied in ....

WAR PHOTOGRAPHER by Carol Ann Duffy

This poem highlights the violence of war and the responses of those who are detached from it. It describes a photographer in his darkroom, developing photographs he has taken in a war zone. The poem is set in a time before digital photography.

All stanzas are **end-stopped**, contributing to sense of calm control, though frequent **enjambment** allows a sense of fluidity

Metaphor links spools of film and pain: emotions are captured in the images

Pattern of **rhyming couplets** reflects photographer's calm control, despite the horrific images he witnesses and captures on film

1   In his darkroom he is finally alone
    with spools of suffering set out in ordered rows.
    The only light is red and softly glows,
    as though this were a church and he
5   a priest preparing to intone a Mass.
    Belfast. Beirut. Phnom Penh. All flesh is grass.

Semantic field of religion suggests photographer's respectful attitude

    He has a job to do. Solutions slop in trays
    beneath his hands, which did not tremble then
    though seem to now. Rural England. Home again
10 to ordinary pain which simple weather can dispel,
    to fields which don't explode beneath the feet
    of running children in a nightmare heat.

Contrast of home and war zone; ordinary problems are easily overcome in the safe environment of home

    Something is happening. A stranger's features
    faintly start to twist before his eyes,
15 a half-formed ghost. He remembers the cries
    of this man's wife, how he sought approval
    without words to do what someone must
    and how the blood stained into foreign dust.

Metaphor for developing photograph evokes a visual image, and a sense of memory

There are few explicit references to the horror of war

    A hundred agonies in black-and-white
20 from which his editor will pick out five or six
    for Sunday's supplement. The reader's eyeballs prick
    with tears between the bath and pre-lunch beers.
    From the aeroplane he stares impassively at where
    he earns his living and they do not care.

Sense of duty: his work is important

Juxtaposition questions how fully the five or six published photographs represent the hundred agonies he has recorded in the war zone

Irony: he feels the people at home are desensitised to his images of suffering

Rhyme trivialises the tears, which are quickly forgotten

Verb suggests a limited emotional reaction in the reader

What is the poem's setting?

- The poem's focus moves between the **photographer's darkroom**, **memories** of the incidents he has photographed, and the **aeroplane** as he looks down and thinks about the people below.

- The **peace** of home in **'Rural England'** is **contrasted** with the **violence and fear** of a war zone.

What is the poem about?

- A war photographer is in a **darkroom**, developing his photographs from a war zone.

- The photographs prompt **memories** of the incidents he has photographed.

- Only a handful of his photographs will be published in a magazine, suggesting this gives an **incomplete picture** of people's suffering and the photographer's experiences.

- The **readers' emotions** will be only briefly stirred by the images, and then forgotten.

- The **theme** of **conflict** is explored in the **depiction of suffering**, which is juxtaposed with, and strengthened by, the **mild response of readers** looking at the published photographs.

Five key things about the language

1. The religious semantic field in the first stanza suggests the photographer's solemnity in his work.

2. The suffering and pain of war is implied in fleeting **images** of war, suggesting photographs: a woman's **'cries'** and **'running children in a nightmare heat'**.

3. The listing of war zones (**'Belfast. Beirut. Phnom Penh.'**) could suggest that each is like the other to the photographer.

4. Duffy suggests the photographer hides his emotions: his hands **'tremble'** as he develops the photographs, but not when he takes them; he stares **'impassively'** from the aeroplane.

5. She suggests only a short-lived, mild emotional response in readers of the magazine where his photographs are published.

Five key quotations

1. Religion: **'All flesh is grass'** (l. 6). This biblical quotation suggests the inevitability of death, implying an unemotional response in the war photographer to the incidents he witnesses.

2. Home: **'fields which don't explode beneath the feet'** (l. 11). The comfort and predictability is contrasted with the risk of minefields.

3. Memory: **'a half-formed ghost'** (l. 15). The **metaphor** suggests a developing photograph and an emerging memory prompted by the photograph; also **connotations** of death.

4. Suffering: **'A hundred agonies in black-and-white'** (l. 19). The **noun** 'agonies' conveys the suffering of war; the number suggests its scale.

5. Limited impact: **'The reader's eyeballs prick/ with tears between the bath and pre-lunch beers'** (ll. 21–2). The image suggests the photographer's work is soon forgotten.

Note it!

Compare Duffy's depiction of attitudes to war with the reaction demanded in 'The Charge of the Light Brigade'. How might readers respond differently to the poems?

Exam focus

How can I write about Duffy's use of imagery? (AO2)

You can comment on the images used by Duffy to explore different attitudes to war.

Duffy sums up the photographs in one short, powerful phrase: 'A hundred agonies in black-and-white'. The number 'A hundred' suggests the amount of suffering he has photographed while the word 'agonies' bluntly focuses the reader's attention on the impact of war. However, by using the word 'impassively' she suggests the photographer has to adjust to home again where people don't understand the war.

Annotation
Topic sentence makes clear point about the theme of attitudes to war
Carefully chosen evidence supports the point being made
Signals a contrast within the poem
Further analysis showing understanding of complex issues

Now you try!

Finish this paragraph about another theme. Use one of the quotations from the list.

The poet suggests that the photographs have only a limited impact on the public. This is implied in ....

My progress   Needs more work ☐   Getting there ☐   Sorted! ☐

SPECIAL FOCUS 5: Form and structure

What are form and structure?

- The **form** of a poem is the **type** of poem it is, e.g. **sonnet**, **free verse**.
- The **structure** of a poem is created through the **progression of** the poet's **ideas**, and how they use the form, e.g. **rhyme**, line length.

How do I identify these in a poem like 'War Photographer'?

- Explore **how** and **why** a poet may have used a **particular form**: what connotations does the form have? Does the poet stick to the 'rules'?
- Consider **line lengths**, especially in **free verse**, e.g. how long lines of even length in 'War Photographer' create a slower pace and reflective **mood**.
- Think about the overall 'shape' or **structure** of the poem, looking for **narrative development** or **repetition**, e.g. how Duffy's focus widens out from the small darkroom to the view from the aeroplane.
- Consider the **rhyme scheme**: is it obvious? Does the poet use **enjambment** or **end-stopped** lines, e.g. the end of each stanza in 'War Photographer'?
- Look at the **metre**: what kind of **rhythm** and pace has the poet created – fast, slow or upbeat? **Regular** or **irregular**?

Exam focus

How can I write about form and structure?

Be careful: it's more important to explore *how* form and structure are used than to identify types of form and structure.

Duffy has structured the poem in lines of even length, —————— Form/structure words
creating a slow pace and reflective mood, suggesting
the photographer's calm professionalism. However, —————— Evidence from the
each stanza ends with an end-stopped rhyming couplet, ————— poem
to add dramatic emphasis to the poem's key ideas, ————
focusing the reader's attention on death and suffering in —————— Effect of the poet's
war, and people's desensitisation to it. structural choices

Now you try!

Think about the other poems in the collection in which the structure is significant. What techniques are used in these poems to create emphasis?

My progress   Needs more work ☐   Getting there ☐   Sorted! ☐

TISSUE by Imtiaz Dharker

This is a complex poem exploring the power of paper, its impact on our lives and its fragility. It also creates a connection between tissue paper and human tissue, suggesting the power and fragility of life.

Modal verb of possibility

Link between tissue and paper

Semantic field of light used throughout

Images of permanence and impermanence throughout

Long sentences and **enjambment** create a slow pace and reflective **mood**

Few **personal pronouns** are used, creating a detached **tone**

Paper has power: it stores precious family records

Life is short, but paper can endure for generations

Repetition of 'and' slows pace, suggesting care and respect

Implied comparison signals a developing link between fragile paper and permanent buildings

Alliteration of 'r' and 'm' emphasise and link the permanence of the natural world and human activity

1 Paper that lets the light
Shine through, this
is what could alter things.
Paper thinned by age or touching,

5 the kind you find in well-used books,
the back of the Koran, where a hand
has written in the names and histories,
who was born to whom,

the height and weight, who
10 died where and how, on which sepia date,
pages smoothed and stroked and turned
transparent with attention.

If buildings were paper, I might
feel their drift, see how easily
15 they fall away on a sigh, a shift
in the direction of the wind.

Maps too. The sun shines through
their borderlines, the marks
that rivers make, roads,
20 railtracks, mountainfolds,

Adjective suggest thinness and fragility, in contrast to the power of paper and money to control our lives

Fine slips from grocery shops
that say how much was sold
and what was paid by credit card
might fly our lives like paper kites.

Image of a paper kite in this **simile** highlights the fragility and power of paper

25 An architect could use all this,
place layer over layer, luminous
script over numbers over line,
and never wish to build again with brick

Repetition of 'over' creates the impression of building with layers of paper

or block, but let the daylight break
30 through capitals and monoliths,
through the shapes that pride can make,
find a way to trace a grand design

Enjambment gives this phrase emphasis

with living tissue, raise a structure
never meant to last,
35 of paper smoothed and stroked
and thinned to be transparent,

Human arrogance: shown through buildings that are built to last

turned into your skin.

Adjective links flesh and paper

Single line **stanza** gives weight and emphasis to this final idea

Link between tissue paper and human tissue

Echoes line 11, but now highlights the fragility of paper in the **verb** 'thinned'

TISSUE by Imtiaz Dharker

What is the poem's setting?

- The focus of the poem **shifts** constantly from intimate **images of a family** poring over the **family Koran**, to more dramatic **images of maps** showing borderlines, roads and rivers, to an **architect** at work, to **cityscapes** of buildings.

- Within each image, references to **permanence** and **impermanence** highlight the poem's shifting focus and the nature of change.

What is the poem about?

- Dharker explores the **power** and **possibility** in paper to **'alter things'**.

- The **theme** of **power** is shown in the power of paper to record and **dominate** our lives, despite, ironically, its **fragility**.

- The poet suggests the **power of paper records** through the image of a family Koran in which **'names and histories'** are recorded.

- The poet implies the **power and fragility of paper** through the image of a **map**, showing borders and landscapes, but through which **'The sun shines'**.

- The poet links the **physical power of human beings and paper** (implied through reference to **'living tissue'**) and suggests it is greater than the arrogant permanence of buildings.

Five key things about the language

1. **Semantic fields** of light, nature, construction, permanence and impermanence link ideas **ambiguously** in this complex poem.

2. The poem explores possibilities, using **modal verbs** (**'might'**, **'could'**) and **conditional clauses**, such as **'If buildings were paper'**.

3. Infrequent use of personal pronouns (e.g. **'I'**, **'you'**) create a detached **tone**, implying an exploration of universal issues.

4. References to **'Fine slips from grocery shops'** and **'credit card'** imply the power of business and money to dominates our lives.

5. The final image of a **'grand design'**, suggesting a city **'never meant to last'**, built of paper, or human tissue, is highly ambiguous and open to interpretation.

Five key quotations

1. **Fragility of paper:** 'Paper thinned by age or touching' (l. 4). Time and contact slowly destroy paper.

2. **Power of written records:** 'a hand/has written in the names and histories' (ll. 6–7). Our lives are recorded on paper; the **noun** 'hand' helps to create an image of the act of writing.

3. **Power of the natural world:** 'The sun shines through/their borderlines' (ll. 17–18). The natural world overpowers the fragile boundaries and borders that humans impose on it.

4. **Power of money:** 'what was paid by credit card' (l. 23). Our money and spending are recorded on paper.

5. **Fragility and power of human beings:** 'paper …//turned into your skin' (ll. 35–7). Image implies human beings share the fragility and power of paper.

Note it!

Compare Dharker's **viewpoint** on the fragility/power of human beings, with Shelley's viewpoint, explored in 'Ozymandias'. What similarities are there in their explorations of humans recording their achievements?

Exam focus

How can I write about the theme of power?

You can use the images Dharker creates to explore the power of paper.

Dharker suggests a vivid image of a family gathered around their family Koran, turning the pages and exploring the 'names and histories' that 'a hand' has recorded there. The noun 'hand' creates an image of someone writing, using paper to record people's lives, while the adjective 'sepia' suggests records dating back years through the family's history and the fading strength of the paper.	Topic sentence makes clear point about the theme of power
	Carefully chosen words all support the point being made
	Signals a linked, developed analysis
	Further exploration of the image created, linked to the topic sentence and theme

Now you try!

Finish this paragraph about another theme. Use one of the quotations from the list.

The poet also suggests the fragility of paper. This is explored through ....

THE EMIGRÉE by Carol Rumens

This poem explores the experience of an emigrée – someone who has had to leave their own country and emigrate to live in another for political reasons, and often as a result of war. It could be read as an exploration of the ability of past experience and memory to overpower the reality of the present.

Childhood memories: language choice suggests a child's story

Possibly a **metaphor** for the coldness of war and tyranny, in contrast to the sunlight of the speaker's memories

Metaphor implies solidity, beauty and colour

1 There once was a country … I left it as a child
  but my memory of it is sunlight-clear
  for it seems I never saw it in that November
  which, I am told, comes to the mildest city.
5 The worst news I receive of it cannot break
  my original view, the bright, filled paperweight.
  It may be at war, it may be sick with tyrants,
  but I am branded by an impression of sunlight.

  The white streets of that city, the graceful slopes
10 glow even clearer as time rolls its tanks
  and the frontiers rise between us, close like waves.
  That child's vocabulary I carried here
  like a hollow doll, opens and spills a grammar.
  Soon I shall have every coloured molecule of it.
15 It may by now be a lie, banned by the state
  but I can't get it off my tongue. It tastes of sunlight.

  I have no passport, there's no way back at all
  but my city comes to me in its own white plane.
  It lies down in front of me, docile as paper;
20 I comb its hair and love its shining eyes.
  My city takes me dancing through the city
  of walls. They accuse me of absence, they circle me.
  They accuse me of being dark in their free city.
  My city hides behind me. They mutter death,
25 and my shadow falls as evidence of sunlight.

Metaphor suggests this impression is permanently burnt into the speaker's mind

Light, purity and innocence of the city (see **adjective** 'white')

Simile of fragility recalls image of an unbreakable paperweight from previous stanza

Metaphor highlights that her language is a permanent part of her

Repetition: this **noun** concludes each stanza: evokes warmth, brightness, joy

Metaphor recalls image of doll on line 13

Personification of the city needing love and care, then bringing joy

Final line of this stanza makes it longer than stanzas 1 and 2, giving emphasis to this final image

Vague **pronoun**: an unnamed, threatening power

What is the poem's setting?

- The poem describes the **city** which the speaker recalls from **childhood**, but which has now been **transformed by war and tyranny**.
- The city is presented as a **place of warmth and happiness**.

What is the poem about?

- The speaker explains that she **left her country when she was a child**.
- She has **strong memories** of her **home** and her **language**. War and distance have failed to break her connection with it, though she can never return there.
- Thoughts of her city bring **joy**.
- Her **'impression of sunlight' cannot be broken** by the **vague and threatening** forces that **'circle'** the speaker in the final stanza.
- The **theme** of **memory** is explored in the **difference** between the **city of the past** that the speaker remembers and the **city of the present** which the speaker imagines.

Five key things about the language

1. Images of light and the noun **'sunlight'** repeat throughout the poem, reflecting the speaker's warm feelings at the memory of her city. In contrast, references to the cold, dark month of **'November'** and shadows suggest the forces that drove her out of her city.

2. Oppressive/militaristic language, e.g. **'time rolls its tanks'**, **'frontiers rise'**, also hints at these forces, while **'spills a grammar'** evokes a breakage or wound.

3. Language choices and imagery focus on exploring the speaker's feelings; there is very little physical description of the city.

4. The key image of a paperweight could suggest a solid, weighty piece of glass in which an image is preserved – or a snow-globe, suggesting a childhood toy and a fragile bubble of glass in which an unrealistic, romanticised model of the city is held, like the speaker's childhood memories.

5. Memory's permanence is shown in the speaker's native language which she cannot lose, and the **'impression of sunlight'** which brands her.

Five key quotations

1. A child's story: **'There once was a country'** (l. 1). Suggests a fairy-tale opening, evoking childhood memories.

2. Past and present: **'That child's vocabulary I carried here/like a hollow doll'** (l. 12–13). Language ties her present to her past, and evokes an image of a vulnerable child.

3. Fragile memory: **'I comb its hair and love its shining eyes'** (l. 20). Recalls the hollow doll image, suggesting a fragile memory of a now fragile city which she nurtures.

4. Joy: **'My city takes me dancing through the city'** (l. 21). **Personification** suggests memories of her city bring joy.

5. Light and shadow: **'I am branded by an impression of sunlight'** (l. 8). Frequent references to 'sunlight' have positive **connotations** of warmth, comfort, beauty and happiness.

Note it!

Compare Rumens's exploration of loss, and of the power of memory, with the speaker's thoughts of her son in 'Poppies'. Do the speakers' memories provoke similar feelings?

Exam focus

How can I write about Rumens's use of imagery? AO2

You can comment on her presentation of the theme of memory.

Throughout the poem, Rumens uses the word 'sunlight' to suggest how she remembers the city she was forced to leave. At the end of the first stanza, she implies how strong these memories are: 'I am branded by an impression of sunlight.' The word 'branded' suggests permanence, highlighting the unbreakable link she feels with her city.

Identifies a significant pattern of language choice in the poem

Topic sentence makes clear point about the theme of memory

Carefully chosen quotation supports the point being made

Analyses the writer's language choices in depth and detail

Now you try!

Finish this paragraph about another theme. Use one of the quotations from the list.

The poet suggests that her memories of the city are fragile. This is implied in ....

My progress   Needs more work ☐   Getting there ☐   Sorted! ☐

SPECIAL FOCUS 6: Comparing poems

What do I need to do?

- In **Section B** of your exam paper, you will need to comment on the ways a **given poem** from the cluster, and one of your own choice from the cluster, explore a **specific issue** or **relationship**.

How do I do it?

- **Make** your **choice of poem** quickly but carefully based on the **question**.
- **Annotate** the given poem, and **link** these notes to those on your chosen poem.
- **Decide** on the **aspects** you are going **to compare**, and **structure** your response based on these aspects.
- **Decide** whether you will tackle **one poem** first, **then the other** – or **compare/contrast** ideas as **you go along**.
- **Make clear** what aspect you are tackling at the **start of each paragraph**.
- Use appropriate **comparative** and **contrasting** connective words and phrases to explore ideas (e.g. *in the same way, even though, however*).
- **Synthesise** ideas in order to give **an overview** of aspects of the two poems (e.g. *Both poems use violent imagery …*).

Exam focus

How can I compare two poems?

Look at this example:

> 'Ozymandias' and 'The Emigrée' explore power using very different approaches. Shelley describes the arrogance of the statue's 'sneer of cold command' and its claim to be 'king of kings'. Rumens, however, creates a much vaguer sense of power, using only the pronoun 'they' to suggest the powerful are faceless and use intimidation to achieve control as they 'mutter death'. Shelley describes the arrogance of power, while Rumens suggests the power of threat.

Topic sentence identifies difference	Explores first poem, using carefully selected quotations
	Comparative **adverbial** signals a contrast
	Summarises the key difference, identified in the topic sentence

Now you try!

Write a further paragraph in which you compare or contrast the use of language in these two poems to explore the settings they describe.

CHECKING OUT ME HISTORY by John Agard

This poem is written in a distinctively Caribbean **voice**. It identifies a people's history as being central to their understanding and appreciation of their cultural heritage and identity.

Phonetic spelling showing Caribbean **dialect** to create a clear voice and identity

Pronoun presents those in power as a faceless, nameless force

First person speaker with a strong Caribbean-British voice

History is a construction put together by those in power

1 Dem tell me
  Dem tell me
  Wha dem want to tell me

  Bandage up me eye with me own history
5 Blind me to me own identity

  Dem tell me bout 1066 and all dat
  dem tell me bout Dick Whittington and he cat
  But Toussaint L'Ouverture
  no dem never tell me bout dat

10   Toussaint
     a slave
     with vision
     lick back
     Napoleon
15   battalion
     and first Black
     Republic born
     Toussaint de thorn
     to de French
20   Toussaint de beacon
     of de Haitian Revolution

  Dem tell me bout de man who discover de balloon
  and de cow who jump over de moon
  Dem tell me bout de dish ran away with de spoon
25 but dem never tell me bout Nanny de maroon

Possessive pronouns suggest ownership of history and identity

Metaphor suggests that being denied your history is disabling

British history as a set of dates that everyone is expected to know

History is as untruthful and unreliable as folk tales

Power is maintained by keeping people ignorant of some aspects of history

Repetition suggests relentless drilling with 'British' history

Dry, factual style for British history contrasts with rich **imagery** of Caribbean history

Loose **rhyme** scheme and **free verse** used throughout; however, insistent rhyme here creates a mocking effect

56

Italics and indent used to highlight Caribbean history, written in a more lyrical style

Nanny
see-far woman
of mountain dream
fire-woman struggle
30 *hopeful stream*
to freedom river

Caribbean heroes are metaphorically linked to light

Dem tell me bout Lord Nelson and Waterloo
but dem never tell me bout Shaka de great Zulu
Dem tell me bout Columbus and 1492
35 but what happen to de Caribs and de Arawaks too

Dem tell me bout Florence Nightingale and she lamp
and how Robin Hood used to camp
Dem tell me bout ole King Cole was a merry ole soul
but dem never tell me bout Mary Seacole

Native black history (e.g. Caribs, Zulus) is ignored while white, European figures (Nelson, Columbus) and their achievements are promoted

40 *From Jamaica*
she travel far
to the Crimean War
she volunteer to go
and even when de British said no
45 *she still brave the Russian snow*
a healing star
among the wounded
a yellow sunrise
to the dying

A British-Jamaican woman who pioneered the nursing of wounded soldiers in the Crimean War

Metaphors of hope, rooted in nature, linked to motif of light

50 Dem tell me
Dem tell me wha dem want to tell me
But now I checking out me own history
I carving out me identity

Repetition of lines from stanza 1, but now leads the poem in a new direction

Repetition of pronoun asserts speaker taking control of his education and identity

Metaphor implies the speaker is creating or discovering his own identity

CHECKING OUT ME HISTORY by John Agard

What is the poem's setting?

- The poem implies the **Caribbean-British speaker** has been **educated** in **British schools**.
- The speaker feels that the version of history taught in British schools focuses on **British and European history** and ignores his own **Caribbean heritage**.

What is the poem about?

- The speaker implies that **teachers of history give an incomplete picture**, presenting a history based on what they **'want to tell me'**.

- The speaker lists **examples of the history he has been taught**, focusing on **dates**, well known **British and European figures** and, ironically, **folk tales and nursery rhymes**.
- He gives information about **key figures in Caribbean history** who have been **ignored** in the version of history he has been taught.

- Finally, the speaker declares he is **discovering his own history**, allowing him to **realise his own identity**.
- The **theme** of **power** is explored in the impact of education on the speaker. He feels that the selective version of history he has been taught **'Blind me to me own identity'**, suggesting an **attempt to control or suppress that sense of identity**.

Five key things about the language

1. The poem is written in Caribbean dialect, creating a strong **voice** and sense of identity.
2. It is written in the first person, suggesting an expression of personal experience and opinion.
3. The **pronoun 'dem'** (meaning 'them') and the active **verbs 'Bandage'** and **'Blind'** imply that those in power actively tried to restrict the speaker's access to, and awareness of, Caribbean history.
4. British history is presented as dry and factual: a list of names and dates.
5. The stanzas presenting Caribbean history are far richer in **imagery** and **abstract nouns** from the **semantic fields** of aspiration and inspiration: **'vision'**, **'hopeful'**, **'freedom'**.

Five key quotations

1. Control of information: 'Dem tell me/Wha dem want to tell me' (l. 2–3). Those in power have created a limited version of history.
2. Loss of identity: 'Blind me to me own identity' (l. 5). People's history is a part of their culture and identity.
3. Caribbean history: 'see-far woman/of mountain dream/fire-woman' (l. 27–9). Lyrical imagery is used to present Caribbean figures and their achievements.
4. British history: 'Dem tell me bout Lord Nelson and Waterloo' (l. 32). Facts and names are given in an unengaging list.
5. Taking control: 'I carving out me identity' (l. 53). The speaker can discover his true identity now he understands his own history.

Note it!

Compare Agard's view of his culture and identity with the ideas explored in 'The Emigrée'. Do the poems express similar ideas?

Exam focus

How can I write about the theme of control?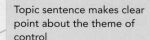

You can explore Agard's **viewpoint** on the role of education.

> The speaker implies that those in power have chosen to teach British history and ignore Caribbean history. For example, he suggests that 'Dem tell me/Wha dem want to tell me'. The verb 'want' implies that the powerful have a purpose in doing this, while the pronoun 'dem' creates the impression of an anonymous, faceless power trying to control what he is taught. This purpose is presented as sinister and disabling in Agard's verb choices of 'bandage' and 'blind'.

Topic sentence makes clear point about the theme of control

Carefully chosen quotation supports the point being made

Signals a development of the analysis

A close focus on language choices, developing the first comment on the quotation

Now you try!

Finish this paragraph about another theme. Use one of the quotations from the list.

The speaker suggests that he has had to take control of his own history and identity. This is powerfully expressed in ....

KAMIKAZE by Beatrice Garland

During the Second World War, Japanese kamikaze (meaning 'divine or spirit wind') pilots were sent on suicide missions to crash their planes into the enemy's naval vessels. This was considered much more effective than any other form of attack.

Ambiguity – may refer to propaganda, prayers, or his own thoughts

Ambiguity – a journey to certain death? Or the chance to be remembered and respected after your death?

1   Her father embarked at sunrise
    with a flask of water, a samurai sword
    in the cockpit, a shaven head
    full of powerful incantations
5   and enough fuel for a one-way
    journey into history

    but half way there, she thought,
    recounting it later to her children,
    he must have looked far down
10 at the little fishing boats
    strung out like bunting
    on a green-blue translucent sea

    and beneath them, arcing in swathes
    like a huge flag waved first one way
15 then the other in a figure of eight,
    the dark shoals of fishes
    flashing silver as their bellies
    swivelled towards the sun

    and remembered how he
20 and his brothers waiting on the shore
    built cairns of pearl-grey pebbles
    to see whose withstood longest
    the turbulent inrush of breakers
    bringing their father's boat safe

A smooth shift in focus in each stanza through use of **enjambment**

Distance, created by using different voices, suggests a story being told

One event has a long-term impact, affecting future generations

Verbs show she is imagining and interpreting his reasons

Simile evokes **image** of celebration

Simile suggests patriotism, pride or celebration

The power of memory

Images suggest the family's closeness, but also fragility

Italics mark shift to the daughter's **voice**, speaking directly to her children

A return to non-italics signals a return to the storyteller's voice

Sensory description emphasises richness of sea-life

Contrast: a richly described image of family unity, then an abrupt change in voice describing the father's rejection by his family

Key turning point marked by new sentence following the poem's first full stop

A culture of shaming those who dishonour their families and themselves

Conforming to society's expectations

25   *– yes, grandfather's boat – safe*
    to the shore, salt-sodden, awash
    with cloud-marked mackerel,
    black crabs, feathery prawns,
    the loose silver of whitebait and once
30   *a tuna, the dark prince, muscular, dangerous.*

    And though he came back
    my mother never spoke again
    in his presence, nor did she meet his eyes
    and the neighbours too, they treated him
35   *as though he no longer existed,*
    only we children still chattered and laughed

    till gradually we too learned
    to be silent, to live as though
    he had never returned, that this
40   *was no longer the father we loved.*
    And sometimes, she said, he must have wondered
    which had been the better way to die.

The daughter implies empathy for her shunned father

A choice of being alienated and shunned (a **metaphorical**, social death) or a literal death

Reported speech creates a further layer of distance

KAMIKAZE by Beatrice Garland

What is the poem's setting?

- The events described take place in **Japan** before, during and after the **Second World War**, when the concept of **honour** was highly valued – and those who behaved dishonourably were regarded as shameful.
- The poem includes a description of the **speaker's father** and his brothers waiting for their own father's return from a successful fishing trip: an image of **family unity** before the war.

What is the poem about?

- A girl's father is sent on a **kamikaze mission**.

- The girl imagines that her father saw **fishing boats** as he flew over the sea and was **reminded of his family**.
- She imagines that this prompted him to **turn his plane around** and fly back home, **failing in his mission**.
- His **wife** and his **neighbours did not speak in his presence again**. His children soon learned to do the same.
- The **theme** of **social structures and attitudes** is expressed in the father's alienation, demanded by the strict values of Japanese society.

Five key things about the language

1. The details highlighted in the first stanza suggest the ritualistic aspect and expectations of a kamikaze: **'a samurai sword'**, **'powerful incantations'**, **'a one-way/journey into history'**.
2. The vivid and richly described image of the fishing trip evokes a powerful sense of place and family unity.
3. **Similes** describing fishing boats and fish (**'like bunting'**, **'like a huge flag'**) evoke feelings of celebration and joy.
4. The vibrant vocabulary and **imagery** describing family life and sea life are in strong contrast to the far plainer language of the daughter's **voice**, recounting the family's treatment of her father.
5. The final line considers the two deaths the father faced: death with honour in war, or the slow shameful death of rejection.

Five key quotations

1. Death: 'a one-way/journey into history' (l. 5–6). The speaker suggests an honourable death brings lasting respect.
2. Life: 'fishes/flashing silver as their bellies/swivelled towards the sun' (l. 16–18). **Alliteration** helps to create a sense of movement and life.
3. Memory: 'he/and his brothers waiting on the shore/built cairns of pearl-grey pebbles' (l. 19 –21). An image of unity, although 'cairns' has overtones of death and burial.
4. Alienation: *'they treated him/as though he no longer existed'* (l. 34–5). Highlights loss of his family life and his social exclusion.
5. His choice: 'he must have wondered/which had been the better way to die' (l. 41–2). The verb 'must have' implies the daughter understands how her father felt at this time.

Note it!

Compare how attitudes to war are shown in 'Kamikaze' and in 'The Charge of the Light Brigade'. How does each present expectations of a willingness to die?

Exam focus

How can I write about the theme of society's expectations? (AO1)

You can consider Garland's presentation of the father's failed kamikaze flight.

Garland implies society's expectations of kamikaze pilots in the first stanza: they are expected to welcome the opportunity to make 'a one-way/journey into history'. Garland's choice of the word 'history' gives this journey connotations of importance, respect and admiration. However, it could also bluntly suggest death in war. This contributes to an ambiguous viewpoint, linking society's expectations and the father's decision to reject them.

- Makes a clear point about the theme of society's expectations
- Carefully chosen quotation supports the point being made
- Signals an alternative interpretation of the idea
- Explores the implications of the two possible interpretations

Now you try!

Finish this paragraph about another theme. Use one of the quotations from the list.

The poet also explores the power of memory and how it can affect the decisions people make. This is implied when ....

1. Look at this ideas map representing 'Ozymandias'. Is there anything else you could add?

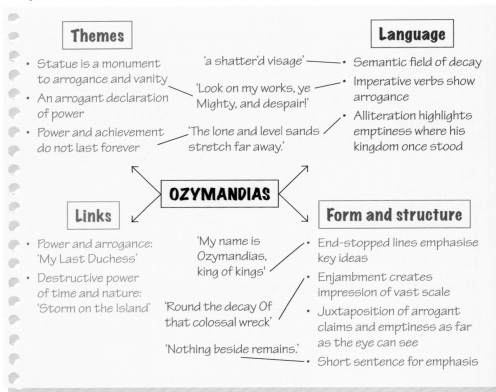

Themes
- Statue is a monument to arrogance and vanity
- An arrogant declaration of power
- Power and achievement do not last forever

'a shatter'd visage'

'Look on my works, ye Mighty, and despair!'

'The lone and level sands stretch far away.'

Language
- Semantic field of decay
- Imperative verbs show arrogance
- Alliteration highlights emptiness where his kingdom once stood

OZYMANDIAS

Links
- Power and arrogance: 'My Last Duchess'
- Destructive power of time and nature: 'Storm on the Island'

'My name is Ozymandias, king of kings'

'Round the decay Of that colossal wreck'

'Nothing beside remains.'

Form and structure
- End-stopped lines emphasise key ideas
- Enjambment creates impression of vast scale
- Juxtaposition of arrogant claims and emptiness as far as the eye can see
- Short sentence for emphasis

2. Create your own ideas map for one of the other poems from the cluster.

Quick quiz

1. Who saw and describes the remains of the statue of Ozymandias?

2. What marks does the speaker see on people's faces in 'London'?

3. What does the speaker in 'Extract from The Prelude' find so disturbing?

4. Name one thing that gives the Duchess pleasure in 'My Last Duchess'.

5. What two artworks does the Duke draw attention to in 'My Last Duchess'?

6. How many soldiers rode into the 'valley of Death' in 'The Charge of the Light Brigade'?

7. How does Tennyson emphasise the number of cannons firing at the soldiers in 'The Charge of the Light Brigade'?

8. In which two seasons do the events described in 'Exposure' take place?

9. What is described as 'a huge nothing' in 'Storm on the Island'?

10. What animal does the soldier see dying in 'Bayonet Charge'?

11. What emotion does the soldier experience in 'Remains'?

12. What technique does Armitage use to create the **voice** of the soldier in 'Remains'?

13. What does the mother pin on her son's lapel in 'Poppies'?

14. What is the setting of the first three stanzas of 'War Photographer'?

15. What are the two suggested meanings of the title 'Tissue'?

16. What is the main impression the speaker has of the city she has left behind in 'The Emigrée'?

17. Name a figure from British history in 'Checking Out Me History'.

18. Name a figure from Caribbean history in 'Checking Out Me History'.

19. What sight does the speaker imagine caused her father to abort his mission in 'Kamikaze'?

20. Who is first to ignore the father when he returns in 'Kamikaze'?

Power paragraphs

Write a **paragraph** in response to **each of these questions**. Include **one quotation from each poem**.

1. How does Blake use **repetition** in 'London'?

2. What is suggested about the power of memory in the poem title 'Remains'?

Exam practice

How does Owen present the power of nature in 'Exposure'?

Write **two paragraphs** explaining your ideas. You could comment on:

● the threat of nature compared with the threat of war

● Owen's use of **personification**.

THEMES Social structure and control

Five key things about how poets explore social structure and control

1. An **individual's power and control** is explored in poems such as 'Ozymandias' and 'My Last Duchess'.
2. The **power structures of countries** are shown in the **education** choices in 'Checking Out Me History' and the **oppressive regime** in 'The Emigrée'.
3. Some poems explore the impact that **social structure** and **social attitudes** can have, such as Blake's presentation of the lower classes in 'London' or the family in 'Kamikaze'.
4. **Social hierarchies** are reflected in the Duchess's failure to give her husband adequate respect in 'My Last Duchess', and the unquestioning obedience of the soldiers in 'The Charge of the Light Brigade'.
5. The **transience of power** is implied in both 'Ozymandias' and in 'Tissue'.

How are social structures and their power conveyed?

- In 'London', the suffering of the lower classes is highlighted in their '**Marks of weakness, marks of woe**' which, it is implied in '**each chartered street**', '**church**' and '**palace**', are scars caused by those in positions of power.
- In 'Checking Out Me History', Agard shows the power of education to impose an identity on individuals, and to '**Blind**' them to their own identity.
- In 'My Last Duchess', Browning depicts a Duke at the top of a social hierarchy who expects his wife to respect his position in society.

How are power and control conveyed?

- 'The Charge of the Light Brigade' implies the extent of army officers' power and control. The soldiers do not question their orders, even though they know that '**Some one had blunder'd**'.
- In 'My Last Duchess', the Duke's ruthless power is shown in his refusal to '**stoop**' to correcting his wife's behaviour; instead, he gives '**commands**' to have her killed.
- In 'Ozymandias', Shelley implies the use of intimidation to impose power through his description of Ozymandias's '**sneer of cold command**'.
- In 'The Emigrée', the speaker's perceptions of fear and intimidation are suggested as those with power in her city '**circle**' her and '**mutter death**'.

How is the fragility of power and social structure conveyed?

- 'Tissue' uses images linking the fragility of paper to the fragility of physical and social structures: sunlight shining through '**borderlines**' on thin paper maps; daylight breaking through the '**shapes that pride can make**'.
- In 'Ozymandias', his statue has fallen and his kingdom has disappeared; '**Nothing beside remains**', despite his arrogant claims.
- 'Checking Out Me History' highlights the power of the individual to ignore imposed ideas and start '**carving out me identity**'.

Three key quotations

1. Arrogance: '**My name is Ozymandias, king of kings**' ('Ozymandias').
2. Control: '**Dem tell me/Dem tell me**' ('Checking Out Me History').
3. Authority: '**Theirs not to reason why,/Theirs but to do and die**' ('The Charge of the Light Brigade').

Note it!

Some poems explore power and the attitudes of those at the top of the social structure; others show the impact of social structure on those at its lower end.

Exam focus

How can I write about the fragility of power?

You can look at how Shelley uses structure to explore this idea.

Shelley draws attention to the fragility of power. Immediately following Ozymandias's arrogant declaration of power, Shelley directs the reader to the surroundings where, other than the statue, 'Nothing beside remains', suggesting that Ozymandias's achievements have crumbled to dust. This short, blunt sentence gives emphasis to the emptiness of the desert, and the emptiness of Ozymandias's proud boast.	Introduces the core idea
	Apt quotation
	Explains clearly
	Language focus develops and interprets

Now you try!

Write your own paragraph about a different aspect of social structure and control in the cluster. Use one of the given quotations.

THEMES Memories

Five key things about how poets explore memories

1. The **power of memory** to **disturb** is explored in poems such as 'Extract from The Prelude' and 'Remains'.

2. Some poems show people drawing on memories for **support and comfort** when in difficult situations, e.g. 'Poppies' and 'The Emigrée'.

3. **Powerful images** prompt memories in some poems, e.g. the painting in 'My Last Duchess' reminds the Duke of his wife's failings, while images of war in 'War Photographer' bring back memories of conflict zones.

4. Memories are presented as **incomplete** or **unreliable** in poems such as 'The Emigrée' and 'Kamikaze'.

5. The **expectation of being remembered** is shown in 'The Charge of the Light Brigade': the poet calls upon the reader to recall heroic soldiers who fought so bravely. However, 'Ozymandias' shows how even the mightiest achievements can decay and be forgotten.

How is the power of memory conveyed?

- In 'Remains', the soldier's memories of the man he killed are presented as aggressive and disturbing: the image of the man being '**torn apart**' by the soldier's bullets has '**dug in**' to his memory.

- In 'The Emigrée', the speaker uses the power of her memories to overcome distance and change. In her memory, her city is not '**at war**' and '**sick with tyrants**', but full of '**sunlight**'.

- In 'Poppies', the speaker attempts to comfort herself with memories from her absent son's childhood.

How do memories change?

- In 'Poppies', it is suggested that memories of the past can fade and be lost: the image of the son's '**playground voice catching on the wind**' suggests memories are elusive.

- Duffy gives brief '**snapshot**' descriptions of the photographer's memories of his experiences in war zones in 'War Photographer'. In contrast, none of his photographs are described, suggesting that his memories are more vivid than physical images.

- The repeated **imagery** of '**sunlight**' in 'The Emigrée' suggests a memory that has comforted and nourished the speaker since childhood.

68

What different attitudes to memory are conveyed?

- 'The Charge of the Light Brigade', by commemorating the charge, suggests that remembering the '**Noble six hundred**' shows respect and admiration.
- The statue in 'Ozymandias' implies the king's expectation of being remembered, respected and admired for years to come.
- In 'Kamikaze', memories are shown to be unreliable. The daughter remembers the story of '*grandfather's boat*' and how her father was treated after his failed mission; she uses these two memories to imagine a complete story.

Three key quotations

1. Threatening: 'huge and mighty forms, that do not live/Like living men, moved slowly through the mind' ('Extract from Prelude').
2. Comfort: 'the bright, filled paperweight' ('The Emigrée').
3. Powerful: 'near to the knuckle, here and now' ('Remains').

Note it!

Whether presenting them in a positive, negative or neutral light, each one of these poems implies the power of memories.

Exam focus

How can I write about the importance of memories?

You can look at how Rumens uses description and imagery to explore memories.

> Rumens highlights the importance of her memories of the city which she left as a child. She describes her memories using the metaphor of a 'bright, filled paperweight', creating a positive impression of their importance to her. The use of the adjective 'bright' links to the images of sunlight repeated throughout the poem, while 'paperweight' implies they are strong, substantial and useful.

Introduces the core idea

Apt quotation

Explains clearly

Language focus develops and interprets

Now you try!

Write your own paragraph about a different aspect of memory explored in the cluster. Use one of the given quotations.

Five key things about how poets explore responsibility

1. The **responsibilities of the powerful** are implied in 'London' and 'The Charge of the Light Brigade'.

2. Some poems explore the **weight of responsibility**, such as the speaker's feelings in 'Remains' and the photographer's in 'War Photographer'.

3. Some poems reference a **sense of duty**, e.g. the ideals of fighting for King and country in 'Bayonet Charge', and **following orders** without question in 'The Charge of the Light Brigade'.

4. **Positions of responsibility** are **questioned** and **undermined** in 'Checking Out Me History' and 'The Emigrée'.

5. In some poems, the poet **does not apportion blame** or **identify** who might take responsibility, e.g. it is unclear who is responsible for the attitudes to shame shown in 'Kamikaze' or the conditions described in 'Exposure'.

How are the responsibilities of the powerful conveyed?

- In 'London', it is suggested that the '**church**' and '**palace**' take responsibility for '**the chimney-sweeper's cry**' and '**the hapless soldier's sigh**'.

- In 'The Charge of the Light Brigade' there is a brief and very vague reference to '**Some one**' who has '**blunder'd**' in ordering this charge. Responsibility is not the poem's focus.

- In 'Checking Out Me History', it is unclear who is responsible for the speaker's education. They are presented as nameless oppressors, identified only as '**dem**'.

How are feelings of responsibility and duty conveyed?

- In 'Remains', the soldier is haunted by disturbing feelings of responsibility and guilt: '**he's here in my head when I close my eyes**'.

- In 'The Charge of the Light Brigade', the soldiers' duty is highlighted in the repetitive structures of stanza 2: '**Theirs not to reason why,/Theirs but to do and die**'.

- In 'Bayonet Charge', there is a suggestion that the soldiers' duty is to fight for '**King, honour, human dignity**'. However, these are dismissed as '**luxuries**'.

How are those in positions of responsibility questioned?

- In 'London', the speaker implies the Church's failure to respond to **'the chimney-sweeper's cry'** – and that this is **'black'ning'** or staining the church.
- In 'Checking Out Me History', the speaker is able to fight back against those who tried to **'Bandage'** and **'Blind'** him to his history and his identity.
- In 'The Emigrée', the speaker is not intimidated by those who **'mutter death'**; she sees their threatening shadows **'as evidence of sunlight'**.

Three key quotations

1. Duty: **'He has a job to do.'** ('War Photographer').
2. Metaphor for sense of guilt: **'dug in behind enemy lines'** ('Remains').
3. Blame: **'Some one had blunder'd'** ('The Charge of the Light Brigade').

Note it!

A number of the poems in the cluster imply responsibility, but do not directly apportion blame. The poets use **pronouns** such as **'they'** and **'dem'**, presenting those responsible as faceless and impersonal.

Exam focus

How can I write about concealing the identity of those responsible

You can look at how Tennyson uses pronouns to move the focus away from these individuals.

> Tennyson implies that the Light Brigade's fatal charge into the valley of Death was a mistake but he does not make clear who is responsible. He acknowledges that 'Some one had blunder'd' but does not name the person, or even a group of people such as the officers who gave the order to charge. Tennyson uses the impersonal pronoun 'some one' to show that he accepts the charge was a mistake, but hides that person's identity, and instead focuses on the bravery of the soldiers who blindly obeyed and did their duty.

Introduces the core idea

Apt quotation

Explains clearly

Language focus develops and interprets

Now you try!

Write your own paragraph about a different aspect of responsibility explored in the cluster. Use one of the given quotations.

THEMES War

Five key things about how poets explore war

1. **Direct experience** of war is explored in poems such as 'Exposure' and 'Bayonet Charge'.

2. Some poems explore the **viewpoints** of **those who have been left behind**, such as the mother in 'Poppies' or the daughter in 'Kamikaze'.

3. **Attitudes to war** range widely from the **heroic** ('The Charge of the Light Brigade') to **shame or suffering** ('Exposure', 'Remains', 'Kamikaze').

4. **Contrasting voices** (a mother, soldiers, a photographer, etc.) provide **different perspectives** on the impact of war.

5. The **imagery** of war or conflict appears in other poems, e.g. in the militaristic vocabulary of 'Storm on the Island'.

How is the direct experience of war conveyed?

- In 'Exposure', soldiers in the First World War feel detached from the **'dull rumour'** of war, endlessly waiting while **'nothing happens'**.

- In 'Bayonet Charge', a soldier is frozen with uncertainty, then charges on to escape **'that blue crackling air'**.

- In 'Remains', Armitage presents a soldier's experience of killing, and the inescapable feelings of guilt at '**his bloody life in my bloody hands**' that haunt him.

- In 'The Charge of the Light Brigade', Tennyson evokes the atmosphere of the battlefield, the dangers of war and the bravery of the **'Noble six hundred'** who rode '**Into the valley of Death**'.

How is the experience of those who don't fight conveyed?

- In 'Poppies', Weir explores a mother's memories of the day her son left home, sparking memories of his childhood. It is unclear whether he has recently joined the army or is already fighting in a war.

- 'War Photographer' discusses the presentation of the **'agonies'** of war through the media. It shows the **distance** and **desensitisation** that **images of war** can create.

- In 'Kamikaze', Garland explores the shame brought upon families by those who avoid war. She shows how close family and neighbours shun one pilot who chooses to abort his mission due to thoughts of family.

What different attitudes to war are conveyed?

- In 'The Charge of the Light Brigade' the poet highlights the bravery of soldiers who, even though '**Some one had blunder'd**', do not question their orders. They are prepared to '**do and die**'.

- In 'Exposure', Owen emphasises the boredom and anxiety of war as '**love of God seems dying**' and '**The burying-party**' looks for soldiers killed, not by the enemy, but by the conditions they are exposed to.

- 'Bayonet Charge' presents the dangers of battle, the fear of '**running – raw/In raw-seamed hot khaki**' towards the enemy, and the overpowering instinct for survival above all else.

Three key quotations

1. Heroism: '**Into the mouth of Hell/ Rode the six hundred**' ('The Charge of the Light Brigade').
2. Fear: '**a yelling alarm**' ('Bayonet Charge').
3. Guilt: '**even the drink and the drugs won't flush him out**' ('Remains').

Note it!

Which of the poems present the war's experiences and effects, in an entirely positive, or entirely negative light? Which of the poems suggest a range of responses in the voices heard in the poem, and its speaker?

Exam focus

How can I write about direct experience of war? AO1 AO2

You can look at how Tennyson uses imagery to convey the heroism and horror of war.

Tennyson suggests both the horrors of war, and the bravery of those who fight. He describes how 'Into the mouth of Hell/Rode the six hundred', suggesting that the soldiers are fearless. The metaphor 'the mouth of Hell' suggests that the battle is a monster, devouring and destroying the soldiers, while the noun 'Hell' has clearly negative connotations of anguish and suffering.

- Introduces the core idea
- Apt quotation
- Explains clearly
- Language focus develops and interprets

Now you try!

Write your own paragraph about a different attitude to war in the cluster. Use one of the given quotations.

Five key things about how poets explore nature

1. The **beauty of the natural world** is depicted in some poems, e.g. 'Extract from The Prelude' and 'Kamikaze'.
2. Some poems explore the **conflict between man and nature**, e.g. 'Storm on the Island' and 'Extract from The Prelude'.
3. A number of poems depict the sheer **destructive power of nature**, e.g. 'Ozymandias' and 'Storm on the Island'.
4. **Nature** is depicted as **dangerous**, e.g. in the cold weather of 'Exposure' and the mountain in 'Extract from The Prelude'.
5. Nature **imagery** appears in other poems, e.g. in references to sunlight in 'The Emigrée', and to storms in 'The Charge of the Light Brigade'.

How is the destructive power of nature conveyed?

- In 'Storm on the Island', violent imagery depicts the power and aggression of nature: the **'Blast'** of a gale **'pummels'** houses and the sea **'spits like a tame cat/Turned savage'**.
- In 'Exposure' nature is **personified** to highlight the threat it presents to the lives of the soldiers: **'the merciless iced east winds that knive us'**.
- In 'Ozymandias', it is implied that time and nature have destroyed the statue and the works of which its inscription boasts so proudly.
- In 'Extract from The Prelude', Wordsworth depicts the power of nature and human inability to control or dominate it.

How is the beauty of nature conveyed?

- In the first part of the 'Extract from The Prelude', the poet creates a sense of space and beauty, focusing on **'the stars and the grey sky'** and the reflection of the moon in **'Small circles glittering'**.
- In 'Kamikaze', the writer uses rich, sensory language to describe the creatures of the sea: **'feathery prawns,/the loose silver of whitebait'**.
- In 'The Emigrée', sunlight is a **metaphor** implying feelings of happiness, warmth and beauty, in contrast to their opposites implied by the reference to the cold month of November.

HOW is the conflict between man and nature conveyed?

- In 'Extract from The Prelude', the writer uses personification to convey feelings of threat, e.g. when he describes his feeling that the mountain **'Upreared its head'** and **'Strode after me'**.

- In 'Storm on the Island', militaristic language (**'salvo'**, **'Blast'**) is used to imply a battle between humans and the weather.

- In 'Exposure', the writer predicts that the forces of nature, controlled by the hand of God, will kill some of the soldiers that night: **'His frost will fasten on this mud and us'**.

Quick quiz

Answer these quick questions about themes:

1. Who uses their power and position to control people's lives in 'My Last Duchess'?

2. What does Ozymandias's 'sneer of cold command' imply about the way in which the king controlled his people?

3. How does the soldier in 'Remains' try to forget the killing that haunts him?

4. How does the writer of 'The Charge of the Light Brigade' want the soldiers to be remembered?

5. Who or what does Blake imply is responsible for the suffering of the lower classes in 'London'?

6. How does the speaker in 'Checking Out Me History' take on the responsibility of creating his own identity?

7. What attitude to war is presented in 'Bayonet Charge'?

8. What does Owen suggest presents the greatest danger to the soldiers in 'Exposure'?

9. Which natural image implying warmth and happiness is used throughout 'The Emigrée'?

10. What is the first impression of nature created in 'Extract from The Prelude'?

Exam practice

Write a paragraph about one poet's attitude to nature in the cluster. Make sure you **use one quotation**.

EXAM PRACTICE Understanding the exam

Five key things about Paper 1 Section B

1. You will have **one** question on 'Power and Conflict' which will be based on **a poem from the Anthology** which will be **printed** on the **exam paper**, and **another of your choosing** (also from the **Anthology**).

2. You will be asked to **compare** how the **poets** of the given poem and the one you choose **present** ideas on a particular **theme** or **issue**.

3. You will have about **40 minutes** to read and respond to the question.

4. The question is worth **30 marks**.

5. The question assesses **AOs 1**, **2** and **3**. Remember that **AO3** relates to 'context'.

What will a question look like?

You must look at similarities and differences

You must explain the techniques the two poets use

Compare the ways the poets present ideas about the past in 'Remains' and in one other poem from 'Power and Conflict'.

[30 marks]

This is the theme, idea or issue you should look for

This named poem is the one you are given in the exam paper

This other poem is one you should choose from the cluster

Do all questions look the same?

- The question might be worded slightly differently, for example: **Compare how poets present the power of nature in 'Storm on the Island' and in one other poem from 'Power and Conflict'.**

- Whatever the precise wording, you will need to **compare** how **two poets present a theme or idea**, and the **ways** in which they do it, i.e. the **methods/techniques** they use.

What do I need to do to get a good mark?

Use this grid to understand your current level and how to improve it:

	AO1 Read, understand, respond	**AO2** Analyse language, form, structure and effects	**AO3** Show understanding of contexts
High	• You make **precise comparisons** between the **two poems**. Your argument is **well-structured**, with quotations **fluently embedded** in sentences.	• You **analyse** and **interpret** the **methods** the **two poets** use **very effectively**. You explore **thoughtfully** the effects of these on the reader. You show **excellent use** of **poetic terminology**.	• You make **detailed relevant links** between specific elements of the poems and **social, historical contexts** relevant to the **core issue**.
Mid	• You make a **range of references** when comparing the two poems. • You respond in a **clear, logical way** with **relevant quotations** chosen.	• You **explain clearly** some of the methods the poets use, and **some effects** on the reader. • You use **mostly relevant poetic terminology**.	• You show **clear evidence** of understanding **context** which is **linked** to the poems in **places**.
Lower	• You make **some references** to the poems, but in rather a **patchy** way, with **little direct comparison**. • You make **some useful points** but evidence is **not always clear** or **relevant**.	• You make **occasional attempts** to explain the poets' methods but these are **a little unclear**. • You show **some** use of **poetic terminology**.	• You demonstrate **basic awareness** of **context** but **links** to the poems are **undeveloped** and **not always relevant**.

Re-read the question below and the poem it mentions (see page 36).

Compare the ways the poets present ideas about the past in 'Remains' and in one other poem from 'Power and Conflict'.

[30 marks]

Five key stages to follow

1. **Read** the **question**; **highlight** key words.
2. **Choose** the **poem** you will compare/contrast the given poem with.
3. **Annotate** the poem printed **on the exam paper**; and **make notes** on the **second poem**.
4. **Plan** for paragraphs.
5. **Write** your response; **check it** against your plan/notes as you progress.

What should I focus on?

Highlight the **key words**:

Compare the ways the poets present ideas about the past in 'Remains' and in one other poem from 'Power and Conflict'. **[30 marks]**

What do they tell you? You must comment on **both** poems, looking for **similarities** and **differences** with regard to the **theme** of 'the past'. Explain what **methods** each poet uses.

How should I use the given poem?

- Check for any immediate links to the question (e.g. the soldier is remembering a past incident).
- Highlight any words, phrases or methods you could use (e.g. **'End of story'** – hides the truth of the memory).

How do I make notes on the poem I have chosen?

- Find any links between the poem you have chosen and the notes you have made on the given poem.
- Write these as a separate list next to the given poem.

What poetic techniques should I look for?

Look for a range of techniques in both poems. These could include:

- powerful **single words** or **phrases** (**'his bloody life'**)
- distinctive use of **voice** (the soldier's seemingly **colloquial** phrasing)
- aspects of **form** or **structure**; use of **stanzas**, **repetition**, **line length**, **tenses**, etc. (e.g. the progression from past to present, as a memory becomes a living nightmare)
- poetic devices such as **assonance**, **enjambment**, **alliteration**, **imagery**, etc.

How do I structure my response?

- Plan to **write 4–5 points** on **each poem**.
- **Choose a structure** that suits you. You could:

    Option 1: Write about the **first poem in full** then **the second** (but can be more difficult to compare).

    Option 2: Write **alternate paragraphs** with different points on each poem (e.g. Poem A, Poem B, Poem A, Poem B).

    Option 3: Write **paragraphs where you refer between the poems** constantly (e.g. Poem A and B, Poem A and B, etc.).

How do I compare effectively?

If you choose method 3 you will need to compare within paragraphs, choosing appropriate connective words or phrases. For example:

Initially, the speaker in 'Remains' appears relaxed about the past incident. He uses the phrase 'legs it up the road' which creates an informal feeling as if this is an everyday experience he can shrug off. Yet, we later learn it is a matter of life and death. 'Ozymandias' also deals with big issues, and the traveller seems to tell his tale in an equally matter-of-fact way to begin with.

Explains where in poem

Evidence and effect

Connectives draw comparison with second poem

Now you try!

Take the same question (on 'Remains') and choose your own poem to compare. Make notes and plan a response, deciding how you will structure your essay (see the three methods suggested).

What does a Grade 5 answer look like?

Read the task and the poem again, then the sample answer below.

> Compare the ways the poets present ideas about the past in 'Remains' and in one other poem from 'Power and Conflict'. **[30 marks]**

In 'Remains', the soldier is haunted by the past. At first, he describes his memories of killing a looter in a war. He remembers shooting him dead and then the looter being 'carted off in the back of a lorry'. Using informal language like 'carted' suggests he is not upset or bothered about the killing. In contrast, the mother in 'Poppies' is obviously upset when her son leaves home. She describes how she 'steeled the softening/of [her] face'. This suggests she wanted to cry but tried to be hard and strong, like steel. Both speakers remember difficult situations from the past, and neither of them shows their true feelings at first.

> **AO1** Clear statement setting out viewpoint

> **AO2** Close reference to language choice

> **AO1** Clear link between poems

> **AO1** Clearly summarises a similarity

The soldier in 'Remains' then finishes describing his memory of what happened, saying 'End of story, except not really.' The first part of this line uses short words to sound definite, but he then contradicts himself, which shows his confusion about this incident. This is the first sign of the soldier's post-traumatic stress disorder which has been a serious problem for soldiers returning from war zones in the Middle East in the last few years. In 'Poppies', however, the poet focuses on the effect of memories on a mother left behind by a soldier. This shows the impact of war even on those who don't fight.

> **AO3** Relevant contextual point

In the weeks after the killing, the soldier cannot forget what he has done. He describes the dead man's blood on the street: 'His blood-shadow stays on the street'. This is a metaphor which could mean the blood stain on the pavement where the man died. The mother in 'Poppies' also has powerful memories from the past.

> **AO2** Quotation not embedded

> **AO2** Explains quotation but doesn't develop sufficiently.

> **AO1** No significant comparison. Focuses on one poem only

Both 'Remains' and 'Poppies' use metaphors to suggest the impact of the past. In 'Remains', the soldier describes his memory of the past as 'dug in behind enemy lines'. This suggests how unforgettable the past is and uses military language to show how the memory is fighting against him. In 'Poppies', the mother uses a metaphor of a song bird released 'from its cage' to describe her son leaving home. This more positive image suggests her feelings of love but also feelings of sadness and loss.

Paragraph 4

The final images in each poem are the most powerful. In 'Remains', the soldier sums up his feelings in the last line: 'his bloody life in my bloody hands.' This suggests he has blood on his hands and carries the past with him everywhere. The final image in 'Poppies', however, shows the mother wanting to remember happier times. She is hoping to hear her son's 'playground voice' on the wind, suggesting she gets some comfort from happy memories of his childhood. This contrasts with the image of poppies at the start of the poem. These symbolise soldiers who have died because they are used on Remembrance Sunday, suggesting her son has died in a war, making the final image of him in the playground even sadder.

Paragraph 5

Check the skills

Re-read paragraphs four and five of this response and:

● Highlight **comparative points** made about the poems

● Circle any reference to **context**

● Underline any places where the student has made an **interpretation**

Now you try!

Look again at paragraph three and improve it by:

● **Adding a quotation** from the **second poem** to support the comparison point

● **Explaining more clearly** what the 'blood-shadow' **metaphor** suggests about the soldier's thoughts and feelings about the past

● **Improving** the **overall style** by using **connectives** to link or **compare/ contrast points**

What does a Grade 7+ answer look like?

Re-read the task and the poem, then the sample answer below.

Compare the ways the poets present ideas about the past in 'Remains' and in one other poem from 'Power and Conflict'. **[30 marks]**

The first impression Armitage creates of the soldier in 'Remains' is of a man who is simply doing his job. He describes a memory of killing a looter and then how 'One of my mates ... tosses his guts back into his body'. Colloquial language such as 'mates', 'tosses' and 'guts' strongly suggests the soldier's voice, implying that this is just a story of another routine day in the life of a soldier who is immune to the horrors of war. Similarly, in 'Kamikaze', Garland creates the impression of a story of the past being told. However, her language choices create a much more dramatic introduction, for example describing a father taking 'a one-way/journey into history'. This image suggests death, but also the respect and admiration with which history will remember this heroic act.

After telling his story, the soldier in 'Remains' simply and casually states 'End of story'. Ironically, it quickly becomes clear that this is only the beginning of the story as these past events will come to dominate the soldier's life. The poem is taken from a collection called 'The Not Dead'. This title ambiguously refers to those who have survived war, but also suggests, like the title 'Remains', the memories that will not fade and which the soldiers cannot leave behind. Similarly, the events recounted in 'Kamikaze' highlight the lasting impact of decisions taken in war as the failed kamikaze pilot is subjected to the living death of rejection by his wife and children.

AO1 Clear statement of viewpoint

AO2 Close reference to and clear analysis of language choice

AO1 A similarity and difference clearly identified and explored

AO3 Contextual point identified and explored

AO1 A clear link between the context of 'Remains' and the ideas explored in both poems

Both poems use contrast to emphasise the impact that the past can have on people's lives. In 'Remains', for example, Armitage contrasts the casual tone of the first half with the dramatic imagery of the second half to add impact to the soldier's suffering. Similarly, in 'Kamikaze', there is a sharp contrast between two different pasts. Firstly, the writer richly describes memories of a fishing trip, when the grandfather's boat returned 'safe/to the shore, salt-sodden, awash/with cloud-marked mackerel'. The use of sibilance and alliteration highlights this safe return and suggests a sense of excitement which only adds to the reader's shock when it is contrasted with the father's return from his failed kamikaze mission, described in blunt, casual language: 'they treated him/as though he no longer existed'.

Paragraph 3

The family's extreme response in 'Kamikaze' is typical of Japanese attitudes at the time of the war, when society dictated standards of honour, and demanded punishment for dishonourable actions. In this sense, the family in the poem is simply acting under the pressure of society's demands. However, ironically, Armitage contradicts society's expectations in 'Remains'. Initially, he suggests soldiers are used to death and it has little effect on them. This is perhaps the attitude expected from tough, battle-hardened soldiers. The second half of the poem, however, reveals that this stereotype is inaccurate: soldiers are as sensitive and vulnerable as any other human being.

Paragraph 4

Check the skills

Re-read paragraphs three and four of this response and:

- Identify any particularly **fluent** or **well-expressed comparisons or contrasts** between the poems
- Find any further references to **context**
- Highlight any places where the student has shown **deeper insight** and offered **original** or particularly **thoughtful** ideas or made interesting **links**

Now you try!

Now, plan and write **two paragraphs** in response to this new task, using the skills you have learned:

Compare how the poets present ideas about power and control in 'Checking Out Me History' and one other poem from 'Power and Conflict'.

- Try to match your paragraphs to the High Level objectives on page 77.

Now you try!

- Decode the question by highlighting the key words.
- Annotate the given poem with points related to the question.
- Choose your second poem and add annotations related to it.
- Plan your points and select your quotations.
- Write your answer.
- Look at the suggested list of key points you could have made in the **Answers** (page 88).

Compare how poets present ideas about society and its structure in 'London' and one other poem from 'Power and Conflict'.

[30 marks]

> I wander through each chartered street,
> Near where the chartered Thames does flow,
> And mark in every face I meet
> Marks of weakness, marks of woe.
>
> 5 In every cry of every man,
> In every infant's cry of fear,
> In every voice, in every ban,
> The mind-forged manacles I hear:
>
> How the chimney-sweeper's cry
> 10 Every black'ning church appalls,
> And the hapless soldier's sigh
> Runs in blood down palace walls.
>
> But most through midnight streets I hear
> How the youthful harlot's curse
> 15 Blasts the new-born infant's tear,
> And blights with plagues the marriage hearse.

GLOSSARY

Literary or language terms	Explanation
abstract noun	a noun that refers to feelings, concepts, states that do not exist physically, e.g. hope, love
adjective	a word used to describe something or somebody, e.g. the red hat
adverb	used to modify a verb, adjective or another adverb, sometimes formed by adding 'ly' to an adjective
alliteration	where the same sound is repeated in a stretch of language, usually at the beginning of words
allusion	reference to something from another text
ambiguity	the quality of having more than one possible meaning or interpretation
article	a word that introduces a noun phrase; can be a definite article ('the') or an indefinite article ('a' or 'an')
assonance	when the same vowel sound appears in the same place in a series of words
blank verse	unrhymed iambic pentameter
caesura	a pause during a line of poetry
clause	a special phrase whose head is a verb. A clause can be a complete sentence
colloquial	the everyday speech used by people in ordinary situations
compound adjective	a single adjective made of more than one word, e.g. four-legged
conditional clause	a clause expressing what might happen if certain conditions are met
conjunction	a word used to link phrases or clauses, e.g. and, but, because, if
connective	word used to link sections of text
connotation	an additional meaning attached to a word in specific circumstances, i.e. what it suggests or implies
dactyl (dactylic metre)	metrical unit of stressed long syllable followed by two unstressed syllables (/xx)
definite article	see article
dialect	accent and vocabulary, varying by region and social background
dialogue	speech and conversation between characters
dimeter	a line of poetry consisting of two metrical feet
direct address	'speaking' directly to an audience, often using the second person pronoun 'you'
dramatic monologue	poetic form written as a character, in which speaker reveals their 'true' character
ellipsis	the omission of words in a line or sentence (…)
emotive	with emotional impact
end-stopping	when punctuation coincides with the end of the poetic line
enjambment	in poetry when a line runs on into the next line without pause, so carrying the thought with it. Sometimes called a run-on line
euphemism	a word or phrase considered more acceptable than an upsetting or offensive word or phrase, e.g. 'passed away' instead of 'died'
exclamatory	expressing surprise or extreme emotion
figurative language	using imagery to write in a non-literal way, e.g. simile, metaphor, personification
foreshadowing	a hint of what is to come in a work of poetry, fiction or drama
free verse	a form of poetry; verses without regular rhythm or pattern, though they may contain some patterns, such as rhyme or repetition
half-rhyme	words that almost rhyme; also called near-rhyme or imperfect rhyme
iamb (iambic metre)	metrical unit consisting of a weak syllable followed by a strong one (x/)
iambic pentameter or tetrameter	poetry consisting of five or four iambic feet per line
idiom	a well-known and widely used phrase whose specific meaning is unclear from its literal meaning, e.g. to bite off more than you can chew
imagery	descriptive language that uses images to make actions, objects and characters more vivid in the reader's mind

Literary or language terms	Explanation
imperative verb	verb form that gives the reader a command or instruction
imperfect rhyme	see half-rhyme
irony	deliberately saying one thing when you mean another, usually in a humorous, sarcastic or sometimes thoughtful way
juxtaposition	putting two things side by side in order to invite comparison
metaphor	when one thing is used to describe another to create a striking or unusual image
metre	the pattern of beat or 'feet' in a line of verse. See also dactyl, iamb, iambic pentameter or tetrameter
modal verb	a type of verb that is used to express possibility or necessity: must, shall, will, could, should, would, can, may and might
mood	the feeling or atmosphere that the reader perceives in response to a text or to a particular point in a text
narrative	a story
noun	a word naming a person, place or object
oxymoron	two contrasting, contrary ideas used to make a point or create ambiguity
person	a poem may use a viewpoint described as either first person (I, we) or third person (he, she, they, it) or, rarely, second person (you)
persona	the speaker of the poem, created by the poet
personal pronoun	a word standing for a person, e.g. I, me, he, him
personification	the treatment or description of an object or idea as if they were human with human feelings and attributes
plosive	consonants beginning with a harsh sound. e.g. p, b, t
possessive pronoun	a pronoun indicating possession, e.g. my, his, her, theirs
prepositional phrase	a phrase fronted by a preposition, e.g. in, with, by
pronoun	a word standing for a noun, e.g. it, I, she, they
refrain	repeated lines or groups of words that convey the same meaning
repetition	repeated words or patterns
reported speech	speech that is summarised or reported rather than quoted using speech marks. Also known as indirect speech
rhetorical (question)	asked for effect rather than for an answer
rhyme	words that rhyme end in the same sound
rhyming couplet	a couplet (two paired lines) that rhymes
rhythm	the 'beat' of a poem
Romantic period	a movement that developed between the end of the eighteenth century and the mid-nineteenth century, emphasising the importance of emotion and nature
semantic field	a set of words grouped by meaning, e.g. bullet, knife, bomb
sibilance	alliteration with only 's' and soft 'c' sounds
simile	when one thing is compared directly with another using 'like' or 'as'
sonnet	a fourteen-line verse, often ending with a rhyming couplet
stanza	a group or pattern of lines forming a verse
synonym	a word with a similar meaning to another, e.g. large, big
tense	the grammatical time frame a text is presented in – past, present or future
theme	an idea running through a work of literature or art
tone	the attitude an author takes towards a subject
verb	a word that expresses an action, state or process
voice	the speaker or narrator of a poem or work of fiction. This persona is created in the speaker's mind, though sometimes it can seem close to the poet's or writer's own voice
viewpoint	the perspective of a poem: the person who is telling it

ANSWERS

Note that the sample paragraphs given here provide only one possible approach to each task. Many other approaches would also be valid and appropriate.

THE POEMS

'Ozymandias' – Now you try! (page 6)
The poet suggests that the power of nature is greater than any human power. This is shown in the final image of the vast desert: 'The lone and level sands stretch far away.'. The poet's use of alliteration highlights the vast emptiness of the landscape, showing how the desert remains but Ozymandias's kingdom has disappeared.

'London' – Now you try! (page 10)
Throughout the poem, Blake highlights the suffering of the people. He describes 'Marks of weakness, marks of woe'. The repetition of 'marks' highlights the impact that this suffering has had. The poem is filled with language choices from the semantic field of unhappiness and pain, creating an overwhelming impression of a city filled with hardship.

Extract from 'The Prelude'– Now you try! (page 15)
The poet also suggests the lasting effect that this disturbing experience of nature had on him. At the end of the poem he describes how 'for many days … mighty forms … moved slowly through the mind'. Again, Wordsworth personifies the mountains, adding to the impression of sinister threat, and highlighting their impact on him. This is further emphasised with a reference to 'dreams', implying that they 'trouble' him day and night.

'My Last Duchess' – Now you try! (page 19)
The Duke makes clear the ways in which his wife failed to meet his expectations of respect. For example, he lists 'all and each' that pleased her: 'The dropping of the daylight', 'cherries', 'the white mule'. This list contrasts the Duke's 'favour' which he clearly thinks should be highly prized, with the works of nature. It implies that the Duke thinks his 'favour' is far more valuable, adding to the reader's impression of his self-centred arrogance.

'The Charge of the Light Brigade' – Now you try! (page 23)
The poet strongly suggests how he feels the reader should respond to the deaths of the soldiers. He does this through the use of an imperative verb: 'Honour the Light Brigade'. This verb is repeated from the previous line, and appears at the very end of the poem. Its position and the repetition are intended to leave a lasting impression on the reader, and no doubt about how they should respond.

'Exposure' – Now you try! (page 27)
The poet focuses on the threat of nature and the soldiers' environment much more closely than the dangers of warfare. This is suggested in the very first line of the poem, where Owen describes 'the merciless iced east winds that knive us'. This use of personification and the adjective 'merciless' present nature as aggressive, dangerous and heartless in its attack on the soldiers. This is contrasted with the way the war is presented as no threat at all in the repetition of the short, emphatic line: 'But nothing happens'.

'Storm on the Island' – Now you try! (page 30)
The poet also suggests that the Irish are used to the harsh weather. This is highlighted in the short emphatic statement at the very beginning of the poem: 'We are prepared', followed by details of the ways in which they are prepared. It implies that the Irish expect and are untroubled by the power of the weather, which is also conveyed in the colloquial, careless tone Heaney creates through phrases such as 'you know what I mean'.

'Bayonet Charge' – Now you try! (page 34)
The poet's use of violent language in the first part of the poem conveys the brutality of the conflict. For example, Hughes describes how 'He lugged a rifle numb as a smashed arm'. The verb 'lugged' suggests the rifle and having to fight are a heavy burden, while 'numb' and 'smashed' could suggest his emotional state. Hughes creates a vivid impression of the impact that war has on soldiers' bodies and minds.

'Remains' – Now you try! (page 39)
The poet also suggests the soldier's feelings of guilt and anger prompted by these memories. This is explored in the final stanza when the soldier describes how they haunt him 'here and now,/his bloody life in my bloody hands'. The constant presence of these thoughts and feelings of guilt are emphasised in the phrase 'here and now', while the repetition of 'bloody' suggests both an angry curse and echoes the looter's 'blood-shadow' that stained the street.

'Poppies' – Now you try! (page 43)
The poet also suggests that the mother has allowed her son his freedom in leaving her. This is implied in the image of the song bird she 'released … from its cage' after her son leaves. The verb 'release' implies freedom, while the noun 'cage'; suggests that her son may have seen his life at home as a kind of prison. However, the image of a song bird suggests the beauty and fragility with which the mother regards her son and her relationship with him.

'War Photographer' – Now you try! (page 46)
The poet suggests that the photographs have only a limited impact on the public. This is implied in the description of the reader's emotional response to the images: Duffy belittles their 'tears', first with the use of the verb 'prick' implying only a limited emotional reaction, then in the phrase 'between the bath and

pre-lunch beers.' The use of alliteration here closely links these two events, implying a very short amount of time.

'Tissue' – Now you try! (page 51)

The poet also suggests the fragility of paper. This is explored through the image of 'Paper thinned by age or touching', suggesting that paper is worn out by use and time. The verb 'thinned' is repeated at the end of the poem, giving greater emphasis to this idea.

'The Emigrée' – Now you try! (page 54)

The poet also suggests that her memories of the city are fragile. This is implied in the image of the city needing love and care: 'I comb its hair and love its shining eyes'. The impression created is of a memory that must be nurtured in order to keep it alive. However, on the next line, Rumens personifies the life and energy of her memories as the city 'takes me dancing through the city'. This suggests that a small amount of care can bring memories back to life instantly.

'Checking Out Me History' – Now you try! (page 59)

The speaker suggests that he has had to take control of his own history and identity. This is powerfully expressed in the final lines where he describes 'carving out me identity'. The verb 'carving' has connotations of sculpture and creation, and of revealing something hidden. The use of the pronouns 'I' and 'me' highlights how the speaker has rejected 'dem' and their teachings in doing this.

'Kamikaze' – Now you try! (page 63)

The poet also explores the power of memory and how it can affect the decisions people make. This is implied when the speaker imagines her father flying over the sea, prompting memories of 'he/and his brothers waiting on the shore' for their father to return from a fishing trip. This simple image of family unity, and the significant decision it leads to, highlights the power of memory and makes his subsequent rejection by his family even more poignant.

Quick revision – Quick quiz (page 64)

1. 'a traveller from an antique land'. 2. Marks of 'weakness' and 'woe'. 3. A mountain: 'a huge peak'. 4. Sunsets, cherries or a white mule. 5. The painting of the Duchess, and a bronze of Neptune. 6. 600. 7. Repetition: 'Cannon to right of them,/Cannon to left of them'. 8. Winter and spring. 9. The wind. 10. A hare. 11. Guilt. 12. Colloquial language. 13. A poppy. 14. A photographer's darkroom. 15. Tissue paper and human tissue. 16. Sunlight. 17. Nelson, Florence Nightingale. 18. Toussaint L'Ouverture, Nanny de maroon, Mary Seacole. 19. Fishing boats and fish in the sea. 20. The speaker's mother: his wife.

Quick revision – Power paragraphs (page 65)

1. Blake uses repetition to highlight the suffering of the people of London. He repeats the word 'mark/s' to highlight how 'weakness' and 'woe' have scarred their faces, and the word 'every' to highlight how widespread this suffering is: it affects 'every man', 'every infant', 'every voice'. The impression created

is of universal misery which, it is implied, is caused by those in power.

2. The title 'Remains' suggests the physical remains of the looter, and the memories that still haunt the soldier who killed him. For example, the soldier describes the dead man as 'dug in behind enemy lines'. Armitage uses a militaristic image, echoing the poem's setting, while the verb 'dug' shows how deeply these memories have affected the soldier. However, the title could also suggest the remains of the soldier, implying that he has been broken by these memories.

Quick revision – Exam practice (page 65)

You could discuss the following:

• War is 'Far off'; 'a dull rumour'; even bullets seem 'Less deadly than the air that shudders black with snow'
• The threat of nature is highlighted through personification; nature is sinister and aggressive: 'Pale flakes with fingering stealth come feeling for our faces'

THEMES

Social structure and control – Now you try! (page 67)

In 'Checking Out Me History', the poet highlights how those who control education have tried to control his identity. He repeats throughout the poem the phrase 'Dem tell me/Dem tell me', implying that he has been told over and over again. This repetition suggests the narrow and monotonous teaching of British history and helps to highlight the figures from Caribbean history that he has not been told about.

Memories – Now you try! (page 69)

Armitage emphasises the permanent effect that the memory of the killing has on the soldier's life in 'Remains'. In the final short stanza, the speaker describes the memory as 'near to the knuckle, here and now', emphasising how painful and unavoidable it is for him. Armitage uses these two colloquial phrases to give the impression of the soldier talking directly to the reader, which adds to the poem's impact.

Responsibility – Now you try! (page 71)

In 'War Photographer', Duffy focuses at first on the photographer in his darkroom and suggests the photographer feels a sense of duty in his work. She contrasts references to war zones with the short sentence, 'He has a job to do.' This could refer to his work in developing his photos, but the phrase 'a job to do' also implies that his work in bringing the horrors of war to the public's attention is a necessity and must be done.

War – Now you try! (page 73)

At the end of 'Bayonet Charge', Hughes focuses the reader's attention on the soldier's fear. He forgets ideals of 'honour, human dignity' and runs with 'a yelling alarm'. This creates a strong impression of shock and panic, suggesting he is running for his life. The noun 'alarm' also has connotations of a signal to alert people to danger, suggesting the soldier is giving out a long, loud noise to signal the need to escape that danger.

ANSWERS

Quick revision – Quick quiz (page 75)

1. The Duke. 2. He used fear and intimidation. 3. He drinks and takes drugs. 4. 'noble'. 5. The church and the palace. 6. He decides to find out about his own history: the history of the Caribbean. 7. The writer implies that survival is the soldiers' main aim. 8. The weather 9. Sunlight. 10. Beauty.

Quick revision – Exam practice (page 75)

In 'Extract from The Prelude' the speaker presents nature as threatening and all powerful. For example, he imagines that he 'struck and struck' with his oars but still the mountain 'Strode after' him. This suggests that he is helpless and powerless to try to challenge the might of nature. The repetition of 'struck' gives a sense of the speaker's desperation, while the threatening image of nature personified implies the pointlessness of trying to dominate or control it.

EXAM PRACTICE

Planning and writing your response – Now you try (page 79)

Answers will vary.

Grade 5 sample response – Check the skills (page 81)

- **Comparative points:** Both 'Remains' and 'Poppies' use metaphors to suggest the impact of the past… The final images in each poem are the most powerful.
- **Context:** These symbolise soldiers who have died because they are used on Remembrance Sunday
- **Interpretation:** This suggests how unforgettable the past is and uses military language to show how the memory is fighting against him; This more positive image suggests her feelings of love but also feelings of sadness and loss; This suggests he has blood on his hands and carries the past with him everywhere; suggesting she gets some comfort from happy memories of his childhood; suggesting her son has died in a war, making the final image of him in the playground even sadder.

Grade 5 sample response – Now you try! (page 81)

In the weeks after the killing, the soldier cannot forget what he has done. He describes the dead man's 'blood-shadow' on the street. This is a metaphor which could mean the blood stain on the pavement where the man died. It also implies that the shadow that the killing casts on the soldier's life. The mother in 'Poppies' also has powerful memories from the past. She remembers wanting to 'play at/being Eskimos like we did when/you were little.' This memory conveys the idea that the past can bring comfort, whereas in 'Remains', the poem shows that the past can disturb and destroy you.

Grade 7+ sample response – Check the skills (page 83)

- **Comparison:** Both poems use contrast to emphasise the impact that the past can have on people's lives; Similarly, in 'Kamikaze', there is a sharp contrast between two different pasts.
- **Context:** The family's extreme response in 'Kamikaze' is typical of Japanese attitudes at the time of the war, when society dictated standards of honour, and demanded punishment for dishonourable actions.
- **Deeper insight:** However, ironically, Armitage contradicts society's expectations in 'Remains'; The second half of the poem, however, makes clear that this stereotype is inaccurate: soldiers are as sensitive and vulnerable as any other human being.

Grade 7+ sample response – Now you try! (page 83)

Example answer:

- In 'Checking Out Me History', the speaker implies that those in power use education to control his identity: 'Blind me to me own identity'.
- Could be linked with the Duke's desire to control his wife in 'My Last Duchess' or the oppressive regime depicted in 'The Emigrée'.
- The speaker rejects education in British history alone, and educates himself to start 'carving out me identity'.
- Could be linked with the speaker's desire to hold on to her identity in 'The Emigrée' or contrasted with the submissive obedience of the soldiers in 'The Charge of the Light Brigade'.

Practice question – Now you try! (page 84)

Example answer:

- AO1: The lower classes are presented as suffering, scarred by 'weakness' and 'woe'; could be linked with the suffering of the ordinary soldiers in 'The Charge of the Light Brigade' or contrasted with the life of pleasure lived by the Duchess in 'My Last Duchess'.
- AO2: Universal suffering of every face seen, highlighted through repetition; could be linked with use of repetition in 'The Charge of the Light Brigade'.
- AO3: Implies responsibility and disinterest of those at the top of the social structure – the church, palace and those who own the 'chartered streets'; could be linked with presentation of the powerful Duke in 'My Last Duchess', or the brief reference to the officers who ordered the charge in 'The Charge of the Light Brigade'.
- AO1: Relentless suffering (despite a reference to possible revolution) implies the powerlessness of the poor; could be linked with the soldiers' blind obedience in 'The Charge of the Light Brigade'.
- AO2: The image of corruption and degradation in the final stanza could be contrasted with the call to honour the soldiers in the final stanza of 'The Charge of the Light Brigade'.